MacBeth King of Scotland and The Clan Finley

As Researched and Compiled by Jacqueli Finley

Table of Contents

PROLOGUE

Per the New World Encyclopedia, Mac Bethad mac Findlaích (Modern Gaelic: MacBheatha mac Fhionnlaigh),(died August 15, 1057), was King of Scots (also known as the King of Alba) from 1040 until his death. He is best known as the subject of William Shakespeare's tragedy Macbeth and the many works it has inspired, although the play is historically inaccurate. Shakespeare' Macbeth immortalized the Scottish king but as a dark, tormented character driven all but insane by his own foul deed, the crime of regicide. Separating the man from the myth is a challenge for any historian. What can be deduced is that he is much more likely to have slain Duncan, his half-brother and predecessor, in battle than to have murdered him. He may well be credited with forging Alba into a viable state, transforming what had been a loose clan confederacy into a nation where people recognized common ties and loyalties across the sparsely populated and often inaccessible hills and vales. As did later Scottish kings, Macbeth appears to have cleverly positioned Scotland between her more powerful neighbors, yet he did not isolate Scotland either. He encouraged trade, improved the kingdom's infrastructure, entered a political alliance with the Holy Roman Empire and strengthened the Church by negotiating a direct relationship with Rome.

MACBETH WAS THE SON of Findláech mac Ruaidrí, Mormaer, or King, of Moray. Many suggest that MacBeth died without issue or sons, but new evidence and research shows us that macBeth did have sons that survived from which many descendants derive and live amongst us today.

MACBETH's death ended a dynasty which began with the earliest foundations of Ireland and Scotland, as we have already seen. At the time of his death, his children were young, so the Clan FIONNLAGH placed his stepson, LULACH, on the throne. However, he reigned only 6 months, being defeated and slain at Eske in Strathbogie by the Saxon invaders and the rebellious adherents of Malcolm CANMORE. After LULACH, no other member of the Clan FIONNLAGH has been on the throne of Scotland to the present day. Members of the clan became hunted outlaws, long before religious persecution drove them from the British Isles.

———

BECAUSE OF THIS THE Clan FIONNLAGH took on the name of the Clan FARQUHARSON, so named because of the Farquhar SHAW of Rothiemurchus. WOOD and FRANCE state: "In 1236 in the Braes of Mar at the head of Aberdeenshire, Scotland, there was a certain chief named FEARCHAR, son of FARQUHAR, who was the fourth son of Shaw DUBH of Rothiemurchus, who was head of a powerful clan known in the Highlands as Clan FIONNLAGH, a sept of the great confederation, Clan CHATTAN, which held large possessions which were acquired by marriage with the heiress of Invercauld and from this FEARCHAR.

———

THE CLAN ALSO TOOK the name of MC EARACHAR or FARQUHARSON. The chiefs were lineal descendants of the ancient Thanes of Ross and Moray, of whom the most famous is MACBETH, the progenitor of this clan. The descendants of this FEARCHAR had moved and settled on the borders of Perth and Angus; some took the name of MC EARACHAR or FARQUHARSON; others, the name of MC FINLAY or FINLAYSON, and of this branch, FINLAY and FINLEY, known as the CLAN FINLEY.

Many wrongly suggested that MacBeth died without sons, Jacqueli Finley claims that MacBeth left young sons at the time of his death at the Battle of Lumphanan, 1057. Under Celtic Brehon Law, these princes were too young to take the Scottish throne, and were passed over in favour of their cousin, Lulach, who was was killed months later by the Saxons who placed Malcom III on the Scottish throne.

———

THE SURNAME FINLEY was first found in Banffshire (Gaelic: Siorrachd Bhanbh), former Scottish county located in the northeasterly Grampian region of Scotland, now of divided between the Council Areas of Moray and Aberdeenshire, where they were descended from the Chiefs of the Clan Farquharson, one of the great federation of 26 Clans, known as the Clan Chattan.

Part 1: In The Beginning

In her unpublished genealogy, written between 1938 and 1941, the late Carrie Alexander WOOD gives quite a detailed sketch of the earliest FINLEY family history. Dating from Adam and Eve, she lists among her sources The Chart of Descent of House of FINLEY, from Manuscript Pedigrees at the Society of Genealogists, London, derived from Annals of Four Masters; CRONNELLY's Irish Families; and KEATING's History of Ireland. Somewhat less detailed, but which would tend to confirm most of WOOD's lineage chart, is a chart entitled, House of FINLEY Traced Back To ADAM and EVE, submitted by Ruth MOORE, with information taken from the Holy Bible and the Pedigree Chart of Queen ELIZABETH and the Royal Family of Great Britain.

This chart can be found on a microfilm entitled, FINLEY Family, which may be obtained from the LDS Church Library in Salt Lake City. The microfilm also contains the entire text of Albert Finley FRANCE's The Clan FINLEY, as compiled by Lillian Hicks FRANDSEN, with additional information added by FRANDSEN. The microfilm may also be leased through Mormon stake libraries by requesting MISC Film Area, #0560192, Item 12 (which means you will have to search through unrelated items on the microfilm until you come to the 12th item, which is the FINLEY section).

According to the Bible, ADAM (meaning "red earth") was the first man and was created on the sixth day. He died when he was 930 years old. EVE was the first "woman," so called because she was taken out of "man," created from ADAM's rib. Tempted by the serpent to eat the forbidden fruit, she and ADAM were cast out of the Garden of Eden.

CAIN was the first child born and later he became a farmer. When God rejected CAIN's first offering in favor of one presented by his brother, ABEL, who was a shepherd, CAIN committed the first murder in history and slew his brother, later moving to the Land of Nod, east of Eden. The Bible identifies one more son of ADAM and EVE by name, SETH, from whom our second generation begins. SETH was born when his father was 130 years old and SETH died at age 912.

Generations 3-9 are as follows: ENOS, b when father was 105, d at 905; CAINAN, b when father was 90, d at 910; MAHALALEEL, b when father was 70, d at 895; JARED, b when father was 65, d at 962; ENOCH, b when father was 162, said to have walked with God for 300 years and when he was 365, disappeared, for God took him; METHUSELAH, b when his father was 65, d at 969, said to have been the oldest person who has ever lived; LAMECH, b when his father was 187, d at 777.

NOAH was born when his father, LAMECH, was 182. He built the Ark and was 600 when it was loaded. When the 40 days and 40 nights of rain began, he was 600 years, 2 months and 17 days old. After the flood, he became a farmer and died at 950. His children identified in the Bible were SHEM, HAM and JAPHETH. It is at this point that WOOD and MOORE's genealogies differ.

WOOD's lineage chart comes through JAPHETH, whose children were GOMER, MAGOG, MADAI, JAVAN, TUBAL, MESHECH and TIRAS. The Bible lists GOMER's children as ASHKENAZ, RIPHATH and TOGARMAH, but WOOD adds BAOTH. She then gives the following outline of the Milesians:

"After the flood, the population of the world assembled to raise the Tower of Babel in 2247 B.C. Of these, the Scythians descended from GOMER settled in the north of Egypt. GOMER's grandson, FENIUS, or PHOENIUSA, son of BAOTH, was King of the Scythians and was a prince who applied himself to the study of letters. He left his kingdom, having placed his son, NIUL, on the throne as Regent.

"During his absence, he proceeded with 72 learned men to the plains of Shenaar and founded a school of languages. While FENIUS presided over his school, his second son, NEULL, was born and on the death of FENIUS, the elder son, NIUL, succeeded to the throne.

"NEULL was left with no riches other than his learning. Therefore, the King of Egypt induced him to go thither to instruct the Egyptians, and was so well satisfied with him, that he gave his daughter, SCOTA, as NEULL's wife. The Godelians, as the people were now called (from GODELAS, son of NEULL), proceeded to a country which the Irish annals named "Gothland," or the country of the Goths, where they remained 150 years before proceeding to Spain."

From NEULL, WOOD's lineage gives generations 16-33 as follows: GAODHAL, a quo the Clann, na GAODHAIL or the Gaels; ASRUTH; SRUTH; HEBER SCUTT (SCOTT); BEOUMAN; OGHAMAN; TAIT; AGNAN; LAMHFIONN; HEBER GLUNFIONN; AGNAN FIONN; FEBRIC GLAS; NENUALL; NUADHAD; ALLADH; ARCADH; DEAGH; and BRATH.

MOORE, as quoted by FRANDSEN, includes the following statement at the end of her chart:

"Queen VICTORIA, by whose command the original compilation of the British Royal Family's Genealogical Chart was made, once expressed the hope that she would be the monarch who would hand over the sceptre when the King of Kings returns. The original chart is in the Library of Windsor Castle. The original copy is in the British Museum."

The chart lists the following generations: ADAM and EVE; SETH; ENOS; CAINAN; MAHALEEL; JARED; ENOCH; METHUSELAH; LAMECH; NOAH; SHEM (note the deviation from WOOD's chart); ARPHAXAD; SALAH; EBER; PELEG; REU; SERUG; NAHOR; TERAH; ABRAM (ABRAHAM); ISSAC; JACOB; JUDAH.

At this point, branches are given from twin sons of JUDAH, ZARAH and PHAREZ. ZARAH's line includes: ETHAN; MAHOL; CALCOL; GADHOL (GAODHAL); EASRU (ASRUTH); SCRU (SRUTH); HEBER SCOT; ROAMHAIN (BEOUMAN); AYBAIMHAIN (OGHAMAN); TAIT; AGHENOIN (AGNAN); LAMH FIONN; HEBER (HEBER GLUNFIONN); AAHNOIN (AGNAN FIONN); EOABHLA GLAS (FEBRIC GLAS); NEIN NUAIL (NENUALL); ALLOID (ALLADH); EARCHADA (ARCADH); DEAGFATHA (DEAGH); BRATHA (BRATH); BREOGAN (BREOGHAN); BILLE (BILE); GALLAM; and EOCHAIDH.

PHAREZ's line is as follows: EZROM; ARAM; AMINADAB; NASHON; SALMON; BOAZ (m RUTH); OBED; JESSE; DAVID; SOLOMON; REHOBOAM; ABIJAM; ASA; JEHOSOPHAT; JEHORAM; AHAZIAH; JOASH; AMAZIAH; UZZIAH (or AZARIAH); JOTHAM; AHAZ; HEZEKIAH; MANASSEH; AMON; JOSIAH; ZEDEKIAH (name changed from MATTANIAH); and TAMAR (TEA TEPHI), who MOORE says m EOCHAIDH (EOCHAIDH BUADHACH; generation 58 on WOOD).

This is where the lines of ZARAH and PHAREZ are said to join together again as EOCHAIDH is said to be ZARAH's descendant and TAMAR is PHAREZ's descendant. Both WOOD and MOORE list UGAINE MOR as the son of EOCHAIDH.

While there seems to be some agreement between the two charts as to generations 1-10 and 16-35, there are major discrepancies in the rest of the lineage. MOORE's lineage chart basically follows the lineage shown in the Bible, as far as PHAREZ's branch is concerned. In fact, in FRANDSEN's narrative, she says the British Royal Family points to their descent through this line as proof of their claim to the throne, through the Davidic Covenant, which states that David's descendants shall forever possess the throne.

WOOD's commentary, on the other hand, continues the lineage through the Milesians, as follows:

"One of the most distinguished princes in the direct line from NEULL was the grandson of DEAGH, BREOGHAN, who defeated the Spaniards in many battles and built a city named Bregantea (afterwards known as Brogansa).

"His grandson, MILESIUS, son of BILE, collected his kinsmen and returned to Scythea and became Prime Minister. His popularity in the sequel excited the king's jealousy and he only escaped death by invading the palace with his faithful Godelians and slaughtering the king.

"Disgusted with the ingratitude of the Scythians, they returned to their fleet and proceeded to the shores of Egypt. Here, MILESIUS soon gained the affection of PHARAOH, who gave MILESIUS his daughter in marriage, who, like the wife of NEULL, bore the name of SCOTA. (It is this SCOTA for whom Scotland is named).

"MILESIUS, after remaining seven years in Egypt, again put to sea and landed at length in northern Spain on the coast of the Bay of Biscay. When the age of the world was 3501 B.C., MILESIUS, a mighty warrior of renown, saw a green island from the top of a tall tower in Spain and chose the most stalwart from among his splendid band of 32 sons to conquer the distant land. They made the dangerous journey in 30 ships, vanquished the race then in possession and seized upon the country, which was divided between HEBER and HEREMON, sons of MILESIUS.

"Irish genealogy begins with this legendary settlement and the four great race stems, to which the leading families of Ireland converge, are HEBER, ITH, IR and HEREMON. It is from HEREMON that the FINLEYs claim ancestry, but it is not until the reign of FEREDACH the Just, 102nd Ard-Rich, or High Monarch of Ireland, that authentic history begins.

"The old and historic name is pure Milesian in origin through the House of HEREMON. Its foundation is co-equal with that of the HyNialls Sept of Ulster, the chief families of which for nearly 600 years ruled as Ard-Rich of Erin (Ireland).

"From HEREMON were descended the kings, nobility and gentry of the kingdoms of Connaught, Dalriada, Idenster, Meath, Orgiall and Ossary; of Scotland since the fifth century; of Ulster since the fourth century; and of England from the reign of King HENRY II, down to the present time.

"He and his brother, HEBER, began to reign in 1699 B.C. and were, jointly, the first monarchs of Ireland. HEBER was slain in 1698 B.C. HEREMON reigned 14 years and died in 1683 B.C."

I would like to add one final note on the line of HEREMON. The time span between MILESIUS' vision and the beginning of the reign of HEREMON and HEBER should be questioned. FRANCE, in his The Clan FINLEY, states that MILESIUS' vision came in 2934 B.C., not in 3501 B.C. as WOOD and

STOUT have claimed. In either case, there is a gap of over 1,000 years between his vision and the time that HEREMON and HEBER began their reign.

Also, consider this: MOORE's chart shows the possibility of a gap between BILLE (BILE on WOOD's chart) and GALLAM (who is not shown on WOOD's chart). GALLAM is said by MOORE to be the son of BILLE, with EOCHAIDH shown as the next generation after GALLAM, but with an arrow bringing EOCHAIDH down to the generation level of TAMAR.

Also confusing is that TAMAR is shown as the daughter of ZEDEKIAH, who, according to a biblical chart that I have, reigned from 598 to 587 B.C. Both WOOD and MOORE show UGAINE MOR (or HUGONY) the Great as the son of EOCHAIDH, but WOOD states UGAINE was slain in 593 B.C., which would put it during the reign of his grandfather.

Another discrepancy is found in the fact that MOORE lists ANGUS the Prolific as son of UGAINE the Great. As seen earlier, WOOD shows UGAINE MOR as generation 59, while AONGUS TUIRMEACH-TEAMRACH, the Prolific, is in generation 66.

So, both charts have some historical corroboration. It is entirely possible that each chart is accurate, with certain exceptions, and chose to go down separate branches, converging at some points and going on separate, but parallel, tracks at other junctions. If any of our members are going to the British Isles, perhaps clues may be found in the original documents to determine the authenticated line. As for now, I will accept WOOD's lineage chart as the proven line until other evidence surfaces.

Part 2: Our Royal Ancestry Of Ireland and Scotland

This section begins with generation 79, as shown in the lineage chart, with the following commentary from WOOD: In the years A.D. 14 to 36, Feredach FION-FEACHTNACH, the True, Just and Sincere, ruled as king, and on his death, was succeeded by his son, Fiacha FIONN OLA (Fiacha of the White Oxen), who had married EITHNE, the daughter of IMGHEAL, King of the Picts. Fiacha lost his throne to ELIM, King of Ulster, who had wrestled the Crown of Ireland from its rightful owners. Young TUATHAL, son of Fiacha, who was looked upon as the next heir, was carried back to Albain (Scotland), where he received the protection of the King of the Picts, his maternal grandfather.

Encouraged by the representation of the Milesians, who had become weary of the reign of ELIM, in A.D. 76, TUATHAL returned to Ireland with a small army raised in Scotland and landed at Jorrus Domhrionn, where he joined his Irish adherents, who had already risen in arms and were plundering the possessions of their enemies.

The young prince lost no time in marching to Tara, where he found the principal men of the Milesian race assembled to welcome him and he was proclaimed King, under the title of Tuathal TEACHTMAR, the Acceptable, or Legitimate. He died A.D. 106 and had married BAIN, daughter of Sgaile BALBH, King of Finland.

Three kings now reigned and slew each other in succession and then came Fedhlimidh (Felim) RACHTMAR, the Legislator, son of Tuathal, and under whom the laws of Ireland were again revised and reformed. He was one of the few Irish kings who was permitted to die in peace, as he died of thirst. He ruled from A.D. 110 to 119 and had married UGHNA, daughter of the King of Denmark.

Then came CONN of the Hundred Battles, son of FEDHLIMIDH, a prince whose long reign was devoted, as his distinctive title imparts, to a series of conflicts. He had married LANDABAND, daughter of CRIMTHAN, King of Leister, Ireland. In A.D. 173, he fell by the hands of assassins. However, from the family of this hero descended the race of chieftains, who, under the title of Dalriadic Kings, supplied Albain, the modern Scotland, with the first Scottish rulers.

CONN was succeeded on the throne by his son-in-law, CONARY II, a descendant of Cairbre FIONN, or CONARY the Great, King of Munster, also of the House of HEREMON, and therefore, of the Milesian race. Cairbre RIADA, son of CONARY II by SARAD (SOADIA), daughter of CONN of the Hundred Battles, in the third century had established the first Irish settlement at Argyleshire, Scotland. He became so important as to find a dynasty. The people governed by his descendants were called Dalriadians and their territory formed the northern part of the present County Antrim, Ireland.

The event of high political importance took place in the fifth century, and this was the establishment under the sons of ERC of the Scotch-Irish monarchy in Albain. The colony planted there by Cairbre RIADA, though constantly fed with supplies from the parent stock, the Dalriadians of Antrim, had run frequent risks of expiration from the superior power of their neighbors, the Picts.

When, therefore, a certain youth called LORNE, noble and with unbounded power, begotten of a race of kings, heard this, that a nameless tribe of his own country was wandering through the vast solitude of Albain, living in misery among the Picts without a ruler, he was stimulated by these exhortations and by ambition of reigning, and aided by the all-powerful influence of the Hy-Niall family, he proceeded to Albain and there constituted himself the first king.

Three brothers who were paramount chiefs in the territory known as the Kingdom of Dalriada, Ireland, LORNE, ANGUS and FERGUS, with a strong army of followers, crossed into Scotland. They were sons of ERC, who was the son of EOCHAIDH the Valiant, who in turn was the son of Colla UAIS, King of Tara, who was the son of Cairbre RIADA.

On leaving Ireland, LORNE, the eldest brother, occupied the territory in western Scotland which still bears his name. He may be counted as the first king, as his reign began in A.D. 470, though his brother, ANGUS, possessed the islands of Islay, Jura and Iona, and other relatives of LORNE were endured.

It was the youngest son, Fergus MC ERC, who succeeded LORNE as king. Though, as we have seen, the eldest brother, LORNE, ruled before him, Fergus holds a more conspicuous position as father of the dynasty, since it was his descendants and not those of LORNE who afterwards ruled in Scotland.

In A.D. 501, Fergus was crowned king and he consolidated the three territories into one kingdom which he named "Dalriada," after his native territory in Ireland. The Lia Fail, or "Stone of Destiny," used in the election of Irish monarchs, was brought from Tara in order that Fergus might be crowned king upon it, and was never taken back to Ireland. Eventually, it was brought to England by EDWARD I in 1300 and deposited in Westminster Abbey. In A.D. 506, Fergus, at a late period of his life, decided to revisit his native country. On the way over, his ship was wrecked, and he drowned. His body drifted ashore on the strand by the rock on which the Castle of Carrickfergus (Rock of Fergus) now stands.

Fergus was succeeded by his son, DOMANGART, who died A.D. 508, and who was succeeded, in turn, by his son, CONGALLUS I (COMGALL), who reigned from A.D. 508 to 537. CONGALLUS was succeeded by his brother, GABHRAN, who reigned A.D. 537 to 560, and who had married LLEIAN, daughter of Brychan BRECHENA, King of Brecknoch, South Wales.

After the Dalriadic Scots had firmly settled in Scotland, their possessions seem to have been divided among four tribes. These were the Cinal Lorne, descended from LORNE; Cinal Gabhran and Cinal Comgall, descended respectively from the two sons of DOMANGART; and the Cinal Angus, descended from ANGUS. Cinal Lorne occupied that part of Argyleshire now known as Lorne; Cinal Gabhran had the district of Argyll proper and Kintyre; Cinal Comgall had the territory of Comgall, now known as Cowal; and Cinal Angus had for its share the islands of Islay, Jura and Iona.

In accordance with the Laws of Tanistry, GABHRAN was succeeded by his nephew, CONALL, son of CONGALLUS I, and who, as King of Dalriada, ruled over the united land of Gabhran and Comgall. In A.D. 574, CONALL died (STOUT names him as CONGALLUS II and lists reign of A.D. 560 to 570) and in the same year, his hosts, led by DUNCAN, his son, were destroyed at the Battle of Delgin against the Picts in Kintyre. It is said the king perished there as well.

This opened the throne to Aedhan MC GABHRAN, son of GABHRAN. St. COLUMBA ordained Aedhan as king at Iona, which was the first consecration of a Christian king in Scotland. This evolution of political events in Britain, Albain and Erin (Ireland) had opened up a brilliant future for the proper man, Aedhan, as the man of destiny.

His lineage was right royal, as on his father's side he had the blood of the Nealls in his veins, and on his mother's side that of King COYL, through LLEIAN, daughter of King BRYCHAN, who gave his name to Brecknoch, South Wales. Aedhan related to one of the three holy families of Britain and also with many powerful reigning families among the Cymry and Gall, who had married the men of the north, Goglia, as the Cymreck bards styled the chieftains who afterwards became the allies of Aedhan when he combined the Dalriadians and Brychans against the Picts of the north.

(Charles HANNA, in The Scotch-Irish Families of America, Vol. I, p. 203, states the following: "Aedan ascended the throne of Dalriada in 574, or perhaps it would be more correct to say he became chief of the Dalriad tribe. In 603, he led a numerous force—recruited largely from the Britons of Strathclyde—against AETHELFRID, the Anglican King of Bernicia.

"Meeting him in Liddesdale, near the frontier line of the kingdoms of Bernicia and Strathclyde [in the present Roxburghshire], a decisive battle was fought at Degsastan, which resulted in the utter defeat and rout of Aedan's army, and the extension of the western boundary of the Anglican kingdom to the River Esk. The annalist, TIGHERNAC, records Aedan's death in 606, at the age of 74.

"He was succeeded by his son, Eocha BUIDHE, who resigned the throne to his son, Conadh CERR. In the year 629, the latter was slain in the Battle of Fedhaeoin, fought in Ireland between the Irish Dalriads and the Irish Picts, or Cruithne. Both parties to this contest received auxiliaries from Scotland. Eocha BUIDHE appears also in this battle, on the side of the Picts, and opposed to his son, CONADH, the leader of the Dalriad Scots. Mr. SKENE infers from this, and other confirmatory circumstances, that Eocha, at this time having withdrawn from Dalriada, must have been ruler of the Galloway Picts. He died later in the same year.

"Domnall BRECC, or BREAC, brother to Conadh CERR, succeeded to the throne of Dalriada on the death of the latter. In 634, he fought the Northumbrians at Calathros (now Callender, in Stirlingshire), and was defeated. Three years later, he was again defeated with great loss in the Battle of Mag Rath in Ireland, whither he had gone as an ally of the Cruithne, or Irish Picts, in their contest with Domnall MAC AED, King of the Irish Dalriads.

In 638, TIGHERNAC records another battle and defeat, being that of Glinnemairison, or Glenmureson, which name has been identified with that of the present Mureston Water, south of the River Almond, in the parishes of Mid and West Calder (Edinburghshire). As the siege of Etin (Edinburgh) is mentioned in the same reference, and as this was the second defeat which the Dalriad king had suffered at the hands of the Angles within the space of four years in contiguous territory, it is to be supposed that these battles may have resulted from the efforts of Domnall BRECC to dispossess the Angles of that portion of their dominions in or near which the battles were fought.

"The Battle of Degsastan, near the Esk, in 603, and these fights on both sides of the Avon in 634 and 638, would seem to fix these streams as at that time marking the extremities of the frontier line between Northumbria and Strathclyde.

"While the Britons were naturally allied with the Scots in these wars against the common enemy of both, it appears that the circumstances of their union were not otherwise sufficiently favorable to insure more than the temporary ascendancy of the Dalriad chief as their leader at this time. It is possible he may have taken the opportunity of his leadership as an occasion for seeking permanent rule. But if this were so, he could not have met with much encouragement from the Britons, for in the year 642, TIGHERNAC tells us he was slain at Strathcawin (or Strath Carron) by OAN, King of the Britons.")

The race of MC GABHRANs experienced repeated reverses. With a feud between the two kindred races of LORNE and FERGUS, the Crown of Dalriada passed for a time to the Clan of LORNE, although it returned to the Clan of GABHRAN upon the death in A.D. 676 of Mailduin, line of FERGUS.

By a revolution, the sceptre was transferred to Fearchar FADA the Long, the great-great grandson of LORNE, and who reigned from A.D. 677 to 697. From his line, some of the most powerful thanes and clans of Scotland trace their descent, with the most famous being MACBETH, who, on his mother's side, is traced back to Aedhan MC GABHRAN.

During the whole of this situation, in A.D. 736, a series of conflicts between the Scots and Picts commenced that ended after a long struggle with alternate success in placing a Scotch-Irish prince on the throne of the Pictish kings. With the expectation of softening by a family alliance the mutual hostility of the two kingdoms, a marriage was contracted between EOCHAID, or AYCHA II, and a Pictish princess, URQUSIA, daughter of URQUIS, King of the Picts. EOCHAID was the son of Aodh FIONN, who ruled from A.D. 748 to 778, and ETHELBAYA, daughter of CATHNEA, King of West Saxon.

However, this marriage led to disputes over succession of the Pictish Crown and in the struggle that followed, ALPIN, son of AYCHA II, who ruled over Scotland Picts from A.D. 833 to 836, was slain in a battle with the Picts on 20 July 836. The whole matter was finally decided by the victory of ALPIN's son, Kenneth MC ALPIN, who urged his rights of inheritance by defeating WRAD, the last of the Pictish monarchs, who died at Fortivet in A.D. 842, in defense of his kingdom. Eight years later, Kenneth MC ALPIN succeeded to the throne, thus uniting Scotland into one kingdom. He had married CINAITH, daughter of ANICUM of the Isles. He was succeeded by his brother, Donald, who died in A.D. 863.

HANNA provides the following commentary on the next few kings:

On Donald's death, CONSTANTINE, the son of KENNETH, came to the throne. After a reign of some 15 years, he was killed in battle with the Norsesmen, who fought the Scots at Inverdufatha (Inverdovet) near the Firth of Forth, in 877. CONSTANTINE was succeeded by his brother, AEDH, or HUGH, who reigned as King of the Picts for one year, when he was killed by his own people. While under the Law of Tanistry, which governed the descent of the crown among the Scots, DONALD, son of CONSTANTINE, was entitled to rule, yet by the Pictish law (Oadh) EACHA (son of CONSTANTINE's sister and of RUN, King of the Britons of Strathclyde) was the next heir, and as the Pictish party at this time seems to have been in the ascendancy, EACHA was made king.

Being too young to reign, however, another king was associated with him as governor. This governor, or regent, was GRIG, or CIRIC, son of DUNGAILE. While the earlier "Pictish Chronicle" gives no account of this reign beyond the statement that after a period of 11 years, EACHA and GRIG were both expelled from the kingdom, the later writers have made a popular hero of GRIG, and his virtues and achievements are magnified to most gigantic proportions. GRIG, having been forced to abdicate, was succeeded in 889 by DONALD (IV), son of CONSTANTINE, who reigned for 11 years. DONALD was also chosen as King of Strathclyde, which henceforth continued to receive its princes from the reigning Scottish family until it was finally merged into the Scottish kingdom.

During DONALD's reign, his kingdom ceased to be called Pictland or Pictavia and became known as the Kingdom of Alban and Albania, and its rulers were no longer called Kings of the Picts, but Kings of Alban. DONALD was slain in battle with the Danes, probably at Dunotter in Kincardineshire.

His successor was CONSTANTINE, son of OADH and great-grandson of Kenneth MC ALPIN, and who ruled from A.D. 900 to 942. CONSTANTINE then became a monk and was succeeded by MALCOLM I, son of DONALD IV, and who ruled from A.D. 943 to 954. MALCOLM I had married BEATRICE of the Isles.

Between A.D. 954 and 971, MALCOLM I was succeeded by INDUFF, son of CONSTANTINE (who became a monk), and then by DUBHE, son of MALCOLM I. KENNETH II, also a son of MALCOLM I, came to the throne in A.D. 971. He came to his end by female treachery, as he was assassinated in A.D. 995 by FENELLA, daughter of CUNCHAR, Thane of Angus.

He was succeeded by another CONSTANTINE, son of CALEN, who, after governing a short time from A.D. 995 to 997, was slain by KENNETH III, son of DUBHE, and who, in turn, was dethroned and slain by MALCOLM II, son of KENNETH II, in 1005.

After the death of MALCOLM II, there was no powerful adult collateral to seize upon the succession. He is said to have provided for this by putting to death the grandson of KENNETH III, who was a brother of GRUOCH, who married MACBETH. This later would come back to haunt MALCOLM II, as we shall see in the next section.

Part 3: The Most Famous Finley Of Them All

Elmer CROCKETT, who lived in Yankton, SD in 1964 (whereabouts unknown today), states the following: "In the year 1009, Momaar FINLEIGH or FINLEY of Moray, father of MACBETH, was the overlord of the tributary of the Manor of Morey or Moray." WOOD quotes the following from Pinkerston's History of Scotland, Vol. II, p. 333: "During this early period in Scotland, there were two kings, for Finlay MC RUAIDHRI, who ruled over western Scotland, was murdered in 1020 to make MALCOLM II the sole king, and when MACBETH, son of FINLAY, succeeded to the throne after the death of DUNCAN, he came into his lawful heritage."

WOOD adds the line of descent of Finlay MC RUDIDHRI or MC RUARI is as follows: son of RUDIDHRI or MC RUARI, who was the son of FERGUS, who ruled in Dalriada from A.D. 778 to 781; and who was the son of EAGEN, who ruled from A.D. 741 to 747; and who was the son of Fearchar FADA, who ruled from A.D. 677 to 695; and who was the son of FERADACH, a powerful chief of Clan LORNE; and who was the son of LORNE, first King of Albain from A.D. 470 to 500.

MALCOLM II, King of Scotland from 1005 to 1034, married as his second wife AELIFU, by whom he had three daughters but no sons. The eldest daughter, BETHOC, or BEATRICE, married CRINAN, Lay Abbott of Kunkeld and head of the House of Atholl. Her son, DUNCAN, was regarded as the king's heir, if not by all of Scotland, at least by the king himself.

The second daughter, ALICE, married SIGURD, Earl of Orkney, who died in 1014. Her son, THORFINN, a boy of 5 at the death of his father, was named Earl of Sutherland and became a powerful Thane of Moray.

The third daughter, DONADA, married Finlay MC RUARI, Earl of Moray, son of MC RUARI, Thane of Moray and Ross, a powerful chief of Clan FIONNLAOICH, who not only ruled over the present Shire of Ross, but over a much larger portion of northwest Scotland.

From Agnes Mure MACKENZIE's The Foundations of Scotland (Edinburgh and London: Oliver and Boyd Ltd., 1957), Second Edition, p. 95 and 96: "The first years of the reign of MALCOLM II were marked by unsuccessful foreign war. FINLAEC of Moray, brother and successor of the Mormaor MAELBRIGHDE, who had been defeated by LIOTR of Orkney, now challenged LIOTR's nephew and successor, Sigurd LODVARSON, to a formal battle. Sigurd accepted, and fighting under a magical raven banner, made by his mother, defeated his challenger. MALCOLM made peace with Sigurd, and gave him the youngest of his three daughters."

However, as WOOD and FRANCE tell us, "Frequent battles followed and FINLAY defeated Sigurd and gained possession of Moray and continued as Mormaer of that district until the year 1020, when he was slain by his nephews, MALCOLM, who died in 1029, and GILLACOMGAIN, who was assassinated by the orders of MALCOLM II in 1032.

"From this union of Princess DONADA, daughter of MALCOLM II, and Finlay MC RUARI, was born ca. 1005, MACBETH, or MacBida MC FINLAY (MACKENZIE calls him MAELBEATHA), who in 1039 became King of Scotland, and who had married earlier, in 1032, GRUOCH, daughter of BODHE and the widow of GILLACOMGAIN. From this line, the FINLAYs and FINLEYs of Scotland are descended.

"WYNTON, the most veracious chronicler of the earlier history of Scotland, styles MACBETH as Thane of Crumbacty, which is Gaelic for Cromarty, where Macbeth Castle stood. The union of Ross and Cromarty under one sheriffdom as at present, seems to be the boundaries of the ancient kingdom.

"GRUOCH (Lady MACBETH) was a lineal descendant of that Kenneth MC ALPIN, who, in the ninth century, had united Scotland into one kingdom. She was the daughter of BODHE, who was the son of KENNETH III, who was the son of DUBHE, who was the son of MALCOLM I, who was the son of DONALD IV, who was the son of CONSTANTINE, who was the son of Kenneth MC ALPIN.

"Her grandfather, KENNETH III, had been dethroned and slain by the cousin now ruling, MALCOLM II, who, having waded through blood to seize the throne, had determined to secure peaceful succession of his own descendants, so since GRUOCH's brother was regarded as the rightful heir under the old laws of Scotland, he had to be assassinated.

"Being merely a woman, GRUOCH was of scant importance, despite her august presence and queenly dignity, so she was left alive to carry her royal blood, her heritage of vengeance, into Moray, where she married GILLACOMGAIN, son of MAELBRIGDI, a powerful chieftain of that district. DUNCAN, MACBETH and THORFINN, three sons of three sisters, were all related to GRUOCH. Her husband, GILLACOMGAIN, was a cousin of MACBETH.

"Presently, another blow was to fall upon GRUOCH as a result of this blood feud, for a punitive party succeeded in pinning her husband into his fortress and fired it, and he was burned to death with some 50 of his men in 1032. By some miracle, GRUOCH escaped, but it is small wonder that the child she carried (MACKENZIE tells us he was later known as LULACH the Fool) became mentally unhinged. She fled from Moray into Ross, filled from crown to toe with cruelty and appealed to MACBETH for help. He, fair, yellow-haired and tall, having some claim to the crown, made his claim effectual by espousing the heiress of line.

"Thus, when death had released the strong grasp of Malcolm II, this lineal race of Kenneth MC ALPIN had become extinct and the succession reverted to DUNCAN, the son of CRINAN, who had married the daughter of MALCOLM II. DUNCAN, the people held, was soft and gentle of nature—strangely different from his cousin MACBETH, who was a valiant gentleman.

"DUNCAN ruled with a light hand and after enjoying the throne for about 5 years, his people took advantage of the absence of THORFINN, Thane of Moray, on an expedition to England, and placing DUNCAN at their head, forced their way into the district of Moray. But the Pictish natives of the north refused to recognize his rights to the crown, and at least looked upon him as an usurper, and headed by MACBETH, attacked DUNCAN in the neighborhood of Elgin, routed his army, and DUNCAN, being severely wounded by MACBETH or his adherents, was carried to Elgin, where he died of his wounds."

MACKENZIE adds the following: "In 1040, the sixth year of DUNCAN's reign, MAELBEATHA carried his wife's feud into action and avenged her brother on his slayer's heir. DUNCAN was killed, not, apparently, by murder at Glamis or Inverness, but in battle at Bothgowanan, and MAELBEATHA took the throne by right of his young stepson, and was accepted, for the only other grown man with any claim was THORFINN of Orkney."

WOOD and FRANCE continue: "No satisfactory evidence exists of the cause of this hostile meeting nor why the king invaded the territory of his sub-king. All this is obscure, but the result is shown by unquestionable evidence existing in the Chronicum Rythmecum, preserved in the Melrose Chronicle and embodied by WYNTON in his early historical works. In a former number of that provincial newspaper, the Kelmarnock Journal, in which a vast mass of interesting antiquarian information is from time to time preserved, there occurred a very learned and ingenuous argument, the object of which was, if not fully to vindicate the character of MACBETH, at least to remove much of the obloquy thrown upon his memory.

"Some historians tell us that MACBETH was a murderer and usurper, and the genius of England's great dramatist has so immortalized the fictions of BOICE, that it is doubtful if ever they will be eradicated from the popular mind. Desirous to arrive at the truth, we have ventured to state what occurs to us to be pretty near the real facts of the case, that DUNCAN was not murdered under trust by MACBETH at Glamis; instead, he died of wounds received in a conflict at a place near Elgin, that he was carried to Elgin by the victor, where he died and that his conqueror transplanted his reamins to the Royal Cemetery at Iona.

"The leniency of MACBETH contrasts to advantage with the bloody steps which marked the descent of MALCOLM II. Even DUNCAN's sons were allowed to escape to England. The death of BANQUO and others are mere fiction of BOICE, originating, no doubt, under the CANMORE rule, being desirous to blacken the reputation of MACBETH.

"MACBETH pursued his success and made himself master of the whole kingdom. He was proclaimed King of the Scots at Scone, under protection of the Clans of Ross and Moray, and representing the northern and Celtic elements of the public by birth and marriage, had the most powerful interests in the country behind him. GRUOCH was Queen of the Scots at last, and her dead brother was avenged, for she sat on the throne in his stead. MACBETH and GRUOCH set themselves to reign well. He made laws for the common will, which were most benign and liberal."

Encyclopedia Britannica, Vol. 6, gives the following insight into MACBETH's reign: "MACBETH's victory in 1045 over a rebel army, perhaps led by DUNCAN's father, CRINAN, near Dunkeld, Perth, may account for the later references (in SHAKESPEARE and others) to Birnam Wood, for the village of Birnam is near the town of Dunkeld. In 1046, SIWARD, Earl of Northumbria, unsuccessfully attempted to dethrone MACBETH in favor of MALCOLM (afterward, King Malcolm III CANMORE), eldest son of DUNCAN I.

"By 1050, MACBETH felt secure enough to leave Scotland for a pilgramage to Rome (MACKENZIE says while there, MACBETH made great gifts to the poor). But in 1054, he was apparently forced by SIWARD to yield part of southern Scotland to MALCOLM. Three years later, MACBETH was killed in battle by MALCOLM, who, as SHAKESPEARE indicates, had assistance from the English. MACBETH was buried on Iona, an island off Scotland's west coast regarded as the resting place of lawful kings, but not of usurpers."

As WOOD and FRANCE state, "His subsequent defeat and death in Aberdeenshire (MACKENZIE says the actual location in Aberdeenshire was Lumphanan on Deeside) on 5 Dec 1057 was calamitous to his family. His clan name ceased and for a time, the FARQUHARSON took its place."

Part 4: Origins of Farquharson

25

MACBETH's death ended a dynasty which began with the earliest foundations of Ireland and Scotland, as we have already seen. At the time of his death, his children were young, so the Clan FIONNLAGH placed his stepson, LULACH, on the throne. However, he reigned only 6 months, being defeated and slain at Eske in Strathbogie by the Saxon invaders and the rebellious adherents of Malcolm CANMORE. After LULACH, no other member of the Clan FIONNLAGH has been on the throne of Scotland to the present day. Members of the clan became hunted outlaws, long before religious persecution drove them from the British Isles.

Because of this the Clan FIONNLAGH took on the name of the Clan FARQUHARSON, so named because of the Farquhar SHAW of Rothiemurchus. WOOD and FRANCE state: "In 1236 in the Braes of Mar at the head of Aberdeenshire, Scotland, there was a certain chief named FEARCHAR, son of FARQUHAR, who was the fourth son of Shaw DUBH of Rothiemurchus, who was head of a powerful clan known in the Highlands as Clan FIONNLAGH, a sept of the great confederation, Clan CHATTAN, which held large possessions which were acquired by marriage with the heiress of Invercauld and from this FEARCHAR.

"The clan also took the name of MC EARACHAR or FARQUHARSON. The chiefs were lineal descendants of the ancient Thanes of Ross and Moray, of whom the most famous is MACBETH, the progenitor of this clan. The descendants of this FEARCHAR had moved and settled on the borders of Perth and Angus; some took the name of MC EARACHAR or FARQUHARSON; others, the name of MC FINLAY or FINLAYSON, and of this branch, FINLAY and FINLEY."

Brig. Gen. (Retired) George HIGGINSON forwarded a copy of an article which appeared in the April 1987 issue of Scottish Field, entitled, "Clan Gathering," by Dr. Emilio COIA and Roddy MARTINE. In it, it states the Clan FARQUHARSON is composed of the septs of COUTTS, FARQUHAR, FINDLAY, FINDLAYSON, GREVSACH, HARDIE, HARDY, LEYS, LYON, MAC CAIG, MAC CARDNEY, MAC

EARACHER, MAC FARQUHAR, MAC GRUAIG, MAC HARDIE, MAC KERRACHER, MACKINLAY, REACH and RIACH.

The article also states: "FARQUHAR, son of Alexander CIAR, third Shaw of Rothiemurchus, is believed to be the ancestor of this clan. His descendants settled in Aberdeenshire, and FARQUHAR's son, DONALD, married Isobel STEWART, heiress of Invercauld. Their son, Finlay MOR, first of the House of FARQUHARSON, fell at the Battle of Pinkie in 1547, fighting for Mary, Queen of Scots."

Donna MC CALLON claims descent from Findlay MOR, although she incorrectly states he was born about 1620, when in fact, his presence as Deputy Royal Standard Bearer at the Battle of Pinkie, where he died, was in 1547.

The Scottish Fieldarticle also gives a brief sketch of Capt. Alwyn Compton FARQUHARSON of Invercauld, who is currently the 16th chief of Clan FARQUHARSON and who owned about 12,000 acres on the River Dee. He states his father's surname was COMPTON, but when he inherited the Invercauld estate, he took his mother's name of FARQUHARSON. He has a twin sister and a brother.

Mary HEPLE also sent an article which appeared in The Weekly Scotsman, on 19 Aug 1965. It refers to Finlay (or Findlay) MOR, translated as the "Big FINLAY," and gives the following history:

"Among the latter-day heroes of the clan were such figures as John FARQUHARSON, third Laird of Invery, known as The Black Colonel.' whose Jacobite exploits are among the legends of Deeside, and who once rode his horse up the steep side of the Pass of Ballater to escape the Hanoverians; John FARQUHARSON of Invercauld, who, as lieutenant-colonel, led four officers and 140 men in the Clan CHATTAN Regiment in the Uprising of 1715 and was captured at Preston, Lancashire.

"But perhaps the most colourful and best known of all was Anne FARQUHARSON of Invercauld, known to historians of the '45 as Colonel Anne' or Lady MACKINTOSH.' She was the wife of Angus or Aeneas MACKINTOSH of Mackintosh, 22nd chief of the MACKINTOSHES of

Moy Hall and Clan CHATTAN. Her husband, accompanied by several men of his clan, was serving the Hanoverian Government in the Black Watch at the time of the last great anti-Union Uprising."

The article goes on to describe how Anne, who was the daughter of FARQUHARSON of Invercauld, used a ruse to save the life of Prince Charles when she was 20 years old, in January 1746. The Hanoverians were gathering their troops to capture or kill the prince, when Anne FARQUHARSON MACKINTOSH gathered a blacksmith and four men and fired weapons into the air, yelling commands which made the Hanoverians think there was a great army present, and causing their defeat.

Part 5: Through The Middle Ages

29

In the above section, there appears to be some inconsistency, which I hope to clear up. WOOD and FRANCE have an heiress of Invercauld in the early 13th century; the Scottish Field article has an heiress of Invercauld in the early 16th century. To further complicate the issue, consider the fact that the lines of descent shown by FRANCE, WOOD and STOUT are each completely different, as follow: At the point in question, FRANCE starts with RORY or RUARI, Thane of Cromarty in 1162; his son, Shaw FARQUHAR of Rothumurchus, Aberdeenshire, Scotland; his grandson, Farquhar SHAW or Shaw DUBH of Aberdeenshire, m the heiress of Invercauld, Aberdeenshire; and his great-grandson, FEARCHAR, Chief of Clan FINLAY, Aberdeenshire, 1236, m daughter of Patrick MC DONACHADH.

WOOD starts with RORY or RUARI MC FINLAY, Thane of Crumbacty (Gaelic for Cromarty), 1100 to 1152; his son, SHAW or Farquhar SHAW of Rothumurchus, ancestor of the FARQUHARSON; his grandson, FEARCHAR, Chief of Clan FIONNLOAH, Aberdeenshire, 1236, m the daughter and heiress of Patrick MAC DONACHADH, ancestor of the ROBERTSON of Lude, by whom he had a large family.

STOUT shows RORY or Ruari MC FINLAY was Thane of Cromarty, 1152; his son, Fergus MC FINLAY, also known as Farquhar SHAW of Rothumerchus, was a tenant of Rossen, Cromarty, 1210, m the heiress of Invercaula, Aberdeenshire; his grandson, Eugenius MC FINLAY, a fourth son, also known as Shaw FARQUHAR(SON), was murdered by WALTER, Seneschal of Scotland, 1223. This is the claimed origin of the Clan FARQUHARSON in Aberdeenshire; his great-grandson, Fearchar MC FINLAY, lived in Aberdeenshire in 1236 and was recognized as the chief of the proscribed Clan FIONNLADH, fourth son of Shaw DUBH of Rothmurchus, m MAC DONACHADH.

As can be seen, there are several inconsistencies, both in spellings of names and in facts. However, careful examination reveals a common thread, and this appears to be the factual record:

(116) Rory or Ruari MC FINLAY, Thane of Crumbacty (Cromarty), 1100 to 1152; (117) Fergus MC FINLAY, fourth son of Rory, and also known as SHAW or Farquhar SHAW of Rothumerches, a tenant of Rossen, Cromarty, 1210; (118) Shaw DUBH, also known as Eugenius MC FINLAY or Shaw FARQUHAR(SON), murdered by WALTER, Seneschal of Scotland, 1223. This is the claimed origin of the Clan FARQUHARSON in Aberdeenshire; (119) FEARCHAR, Chief of Clan FIONNLAGH, lived in the Braes of Mar, the head of Aberdeenshire, Scotland, in 1236, m the daughter and heiress of Patrick MAC DONACHADH, ancestor of ROBERTSON of Lude.

The Scottish Field article would seem to point to later generations of this branch, but I have not seen anything yet which would show the generations in between. However, it does appear that the heiress of Invercauld (unless reference is made to more than one person) did not marry into any of the generations of the 1200s, but rather, should be placed in the early 1500s.

The rest of the records of FRANCE, WOOD and STOUT are fairly consistent, as follows:

The second son of Fearchar MC FINLAY was Archibald FINDLA or FINLAY, who distinguished himself at the Battle of Largs in Ayrshire, Scotland against the Norwegians on 21 Oct 1263. In a charter dated 12 Nov 1314, Archibald FINLAY is mentioned as occupying one-half portion of land in the Parish of Rousnot, Perthshire, Scotland. He married Margaret ROBERTSON, daughter of William ROBERTSON of Lude. Archibald FINLAY evidently died prior to 1337, as on 12 Nov 1337, Margaret FINLAY, relict (widow) of Archibald FINLAY, is mentioned as occupying one-half portion of land in Rousnot. They had three children: Roger, Richard and William.

In a charter of King Robert I in 1323, Roger FINLAY was granted the lands of Clifton in Roxburgh, Scotland, forfeited by Euan DE RUTHERFORD and his sister, Marjorie DE RUTHERFORD. In a charter dated 12 Nov 1342, Richard FINLAY is mentioned as occupying one-half marcate of land in Nether, Balliwich of Cunyngham, Scotland.

The third son of Archibald FINLAY, William, became the Royal Forester of King Robert I. He is mentioned in the Aberdeen Charter No. 18 of the Prior of Rousnot Abbey, concerning the purchase by the king of lands in Rousnot and Perth, acquisition having been made by William FINLAY the Forester and others of the king's tenants in Chuf; confirmed at Dundee, Scotland, 16 Mar 1307. William had married Isabel DEMPSTER, daughter of Thomas DEMPSTER, Laird of Murish, and the former Eleanor FORBES, niece and co-heir of Viscount FORBES. They had two sons; Andrew and John.

There is a Royal Charter of 3 Aug 1366, confirming a Charter of the Prior of Rousnot, stating that Andrew, son of William FINLAY the Forester, and Andrew DEMPSTER, uncle of said Andrew and John FINLAY of Cutlace, partitioners of Menmur, Perth, confirm the annual gift of 8 pounds of goods as tithe of Menmur to the Prior of Rousnot Abbey, given at Kennelli on 8 Oct 1360. The Royal Charter was confirmed at Sane, Scotland on 3 Aug 1366.

Also recorded is a grant of King Robert II to Andrew FINLAY of certain fees for exercising the office of sheriff of Perth, with amercements granted to Andrew and his heirs, to be held as their fee, hereditary forever, confirmed at Kyndroct on 9 Jul 1379. Andrew FINLAY married Marjorie MC DONALD, niece and co-heir of John MC DONALD of Perthshire. Their children were William, John, Andrew and Marjorie.

The latter child, Marjorie FINLAY, married John BALBERNEY on 7 Dec 1394, as in a charter of that date, given in Edinburgh, Scotland, the king confirmed to John BALBERNEY and to Marjorie FINLAY, his wife, the lands of Balberney in Fife, to them jointly and to their heirs (STOUT incorrectly lists the date of the charter as 1428). Her brother, Andrew FINLAY Jr., was witness to a charter dated 15 Jul 1428 (purpose of charter not specified). He married Marjorie BALBERNEY. Another brother, William FINLAY, owned land and houses in Edinburgh, as mentioned in a charter dated there on 2 Sept 1473 (FRANCE says 1476), and confirmed by the king on 27 Oct 1477.

John FINLAY, second son of Andrew FINLAY Sr., became the Bishop of Dumblane in 1406. In 1425, he was the tutor of James, son of Murdoch, Duke of St. Alban's. For these services, he became the Thane of Glentilt and received three devoches of land, to be held by him in fee, heritage forever, for the payment of 11 merks and a carriage of four horses once a year for hunting in the Forest of Bencromby. He married Eleanor STEWART, daughter of John STEWART of Fothergill. Their children were John FINLAY Jr., Andrew, William, Alexander, Robert and Margaret. (Although STOUT lists the life of John FINLAY, Thane of Glentilt, as being from 1356 to 1445, this is incorrect, as both FRANCE and WOOD state he died in 1456.)

There is a record at Logyrate in the Court of JOHN, Earl of Atholl, by which on 29 Jul 1457, he granted to his son, John STEWART, the Thanage of Glentilt, which consisted of 17 townships, and which formerly belonged to John FINLAY Jr., who voluntarily resigned it on 19 Jun 1457 (STOUT incorrectly states that John FINLAY Jr. transferred this land to his son, John). On 29 Jul 1457, John FINLAY Jr. was served, as heir to his father, of the lands of Pebnacrefe in Strothquay, Scotland.

He evidently sold this land or transferred it to his brother, Andrew, as he is represented in the rental books of Cupar Angus, Cistercian Abbey, as living in the township of Kethyk, Cupar Grange, Forfarshire, from 1457 to 1461, having obtained on 10 Oct 1457, 1/12th portion of the Grange for 5 years. He married Mary MAC RAE, who was a widow. As the relict of John FINLAY Jr., she is described on 20 Jan 1462 as obtaining from Cupar Angus Abbey a renewal of 1/12th portion of land in Cupar Grange for 5 years, paying an entry fee of five merks. They had one son, John FYNLAY.

In 1463, John FYNLAY had 1/6th portion of Combryeland in Pentecost, Forfarshire. He figures in different rentals up to 1497. He married Joneta ROGERS (Janet ROGER in STOUT), daughter of William ROGERS. Her father was a renter of Cupar Angus, who in 1454 had leased 1/12th portion of the Grange for 7 years (5 years in FRANCE). He died in 1467 and the lease was renewed the following year by his son, William ROGERS Jr., who died in 1508. His son, William ROGERS III, married Marjory BLAIR, daughter of William BLAIR, Bailiff of Cupar Angus. On 1 May 1542, he obtained from Abbott Donald CAMPBELL a life lease of that portion of land leased by his father and his grandfather. He appears on 23 Apr 1544 as Sheriff Deputy.

John FYNLAY died prior to 1507. His children were John and Andrew FINLEY. On 9 Mar 1507, Joneta FYNLAY, as relict of John FYNLAY, is described as obtaining a lease of a portion of the lands of Downy in the Barony of Glenisla.

John FINLEY was a witness to a charter on 4 Mar 1543 of Father Robert CUNYNHAM, Provincial of the Order of Holy Trinity. The wife of John FINLEY is not known, but in a charter of 2 Jul 1547 to John HAMILTON and his wife, Helen CUNYNHAM, John FINLEY and his sons, Luke, William and William Roger, are mentioned as occupying land in Drumelog and Brintenot in the Barony of Avondale, County Lanark, Scotland. William FINLAY (so spelled in STOUT) married Margaret HAMILTON, daughter of John and Helen CUNYNHAM HAMILTON. William FINLEY became a weaver and settled in Carluke, County Lanark. Their children were John, Thomas, George, William Jr., David and Marion.

David FINLAY moved to Carluke, County Lanark, Scotland, and although his wife is not known, he is known to have had a son, William FINLAY, b Carluke. He later moved to Whitehaven, York, England, and had one son, Edward, b 1759; m 19 Jun 1778 w Mary WILSON.

Andrew FINLEY, son of John and Joneta ROGERS FYNLAY, had, according to the rental books of Cupar Angus, a one-quarter portion of land of Aughenlyth in Pentecost. He figures in different leases up to 1546. In 1507, he appears as Bailiff (Sheriff Deputy) of Cupar Angus, and in 1542, as Sheriff of Cupar Angus.

In the latter capacity, he was associated with Donald and David CAMPBELL, grandsons of the Earl of Argyle. There is a charter of sale in 1491 by Andrew FINLEY to John STEWART of Fothergill of the lands of Achnamarkmore. The seal of John STEWART, Earl of Atholl, and the seal of Andrew FINLEY were appended at Dunkeld on 31 May 1507.

On 13 Aug 1507, there is a charter of sale by Andrew FINLEY to Eleanor, Countess of Atholl, of Kincraigy. There is also a precept of sasene by Andrew FINLEY in favor of Neill STEWART Jr., as son and heir of Neill STEWART of Fothergill, of the lands of Achnamarkmore, given at Glentilt, 4 Jun 1545, in the presence of John FINLEY, son and heir of Andrew FINLEY.

Andrew FINLEY died at Aughenlyth, Forfarshire prior to 27 Apr 1547, as there is a notorial instrument taken by John FINLEY, son and heir of the late Andrew FINLEY, on that date, of the rights and reversion of the lands of Achnamarkmore for 20 pounds, payable in 1 day, between sunrise and sunset. In 1523, Andrew FINLEY married Janet HAY, daughter of John HAY of Erroll, Perthshire, and Janet DOUGLASS, a lineal descendant of William DE HAYA, Cup Bearer to MALCOLM IV. Their children are recorded in the Register of Cupar Angus Abbey.

Their first child, John FINLEY, was baptized 9 Nov 1524. He fought in the Battle of Langside on 13 May 1568. The Battle of Langside, now Battle Abbey, was fought 2 miles from Glasgow, Scotland, and lasted 1 hour. In it, the Regent Moray defeated the forces of Queen Mary. Many who fought in the army of Queen Mary were forced to flee to England and Ireland, and so John FINLEY fled to England, where he died, and was buried in the Parish of Howden, York, on 18 Aug 1578. His wife, Susannah, was buried on 18 May 1591 (WOOD says Susannah was buried 8 May 1591). Their children were Andrew, b 1548, m Mary THOMPSON; Thomas, b 1550, m Sarah MEDWOOD; Christopher, b 1552, m Elizabeth CLARKSON; and Elizabeth, b 1554, m Thomas CLARKSON.

Andrew FINLEY Jr., second son of Andrew and Janet HAY FINLEY, was baptized 6 Mar 1526. His sister, Joneta, was baptized 28 Jan 1529; m Jun 1549 w Thomas BELL of Cupar Angus. The next child, James, was baptized 15 Sept 1530 at Cupar Angus, according to Baron's Court Book, Vol. II, p. 86. This reference also states that prior to 1576, he married Elizabeth WARRENDER, daughter of William and Christina WARRENDER.

The last son of Andrew and Janet HAY FINLEY was Alexander, baptized 27 May 1534. He also fought for Queen Mary at Langside and after the battle, fled to England, then to Killashandra, County Cavan, Ireland, where he died in 1627. Although his wife is not known, it is known that he had a son, Richard, who m Fanny MC DONNELL, who was related to the Earl of Antrim. They had a son, John, b Killashandra; m Mary SAVAGE; who had children: Abraham; John FINLEY Jr., who moved to Scotland; and William, who lived in Dublin, Ireland.

James FINLEY, son of Andrew and Janet HAY FINLEY, and partitioner of Balchrystie, County Fife, Scotland, received a grantor's bond on 27 Jan 1574. In a Royal Charter given at Edinburgh, Scotland on 29 Apr 1574, the king confirmed to James FINLEY, partitioner of Cupar Angus, now partitioner of Balchrystie, County Fife, a moiety of land in Newburn, Parish of St. Andrew, County Fife. James FINLEY's name appears in different leases up to 1596. He died at Newburn on 26 Mar 1597. His children are shown in the baptismal records of St. Andrew's Church as shown below:

Andrew FINLEY was baptized 15 Apr 1576; m Jun 1602 (STOUT incorrectly says 1610) w Christine FORBES, b 1589. Andrew FINLEY d 1654, Newton Rires, County Fife, Scotland. They had one son, Arthur FINLAY, b 1611, Newburn Parish, Balchrystie, County Fife, Scotland; m Margaret BRUCE, who d 1693. They had two children: Christine, and Robert FINLAY, who d 1722 (he appears as XIIc in STOUT, Vol. I, Second Edition, who continues the lines of two of his sons, Robert FINLAY Jr. and John FINLAY).

On 29 Apr 1613, by Royal Charter at Edinburgh, the king confirmed to Andrew FINLEY, partitioner of Balchrystie, a moiety of land in Newton Rires, County Fife, Scotland, which Patrick HUNTAR, son of the late William HUNTAR, with consent of David HUNTAR, apparently resigned.

The second son of James and Elizabeth WARRENDER FINLEY was John, baptized 8 Jun 1579, St. Andrew's Parish, County Fife; d 6 Oct 1670, Incharvie, County Fife. He was known as John of Fife and was a partitioner of Balchrystie, County Fife, in 1629. He inherited land in Incharvie, County Fife, from his brother, James. John FINLEY's name appears in records from 1629 to 1668.

He m Eleanor FORBES, daughter of John FORBES, who d without issue. On 3 Oct 1630, he m Sarah CRAIGIE, who d 1669. She was the daughter of John CRAIGIE (STOUT incorrectly says Hugh CRAIGIE) of Dumbarnie, and

Christine SMYTH, who was the daughter of Patrick SMYTH and Katherine COCHRAN, who in turn, was the daughter of William COCHRAN of Kilmarnoc, Ayrshire, and Lady Grizel GRAHAM, who was the daughter of James, Marquis of Montrose.

Buren's History of Commoners, p. 229, lists the children of John and Sarah CRAIGIE FINLEY: 1. James, bapt. 9 Sept 1631; d 16 Feb 1681; m (1st) 1649 w Barbara HENDERSON, who d 1665 (STOUT says 1658), no issue; m (2nd) 10 Sept 1666 w Margaret MACKIE, who d 1672; 2. Robert, bapt. 4 May 1634; d 1712, County Armagh, Ireland; m Margaret LAUDER; 3. John FINLEY Jr., bapt. 9 Aug 1636; d 1704, County Antrim, Ireland (WOOD says he d 1714); m Jane THOMPSON, who d 1714; 4. Margaret, bapt. 2 Jul 1637; d County Antrim, Ireland; m George THOMPSON; 5. Euphan, bapt. 16 Jun 1639; d 1657.

Christina FINLEY was the third child of James and Elizabeth WARRENDER FINLEY. She was bapt. 6 Aug 1580; m 22 Jun 1602 w Thomas ABERCROMBIE Jr. The fourth child was William FINLEY, bapt. 4 Nov 1582; d 1665, County Antrim, Ireland; followed by James FINLEY Jr., bapt. 25 Oct 1583; d 1620, Incharvie, County Fife, Scotland; m 14 Jul 1603 w Barbara HUNTAR, daughter of William HUNTAR and Grizelda TRAILL.

The last child of James and Elizabeth WARRENDER FINLEY was Alexander, bapt. 10 Nov 1584; d 1644, Stenton, Barony of Abercrombee, County Fife, Scotland; m Grissell HUNTAR, sister of Barbara HUNTAR. The marriage records have been printed by the Scotch Record Society of Edinburgh.

These generations of the 1600s and early 1700s show evidence of the move of the FINLEYs out of Scotland into Ireland and, finally, in the early 1700s, to America. Part of the reason for this was the extreme religious persecution suffered by the Presbyterians in Scotland, as we shall see in the next section.

Part 6: Paying The Price For Religious Freedom

The FINLEYs have always had strong religious beliefs. As we have already seen, one John FINLAY became the Bishop of Dumblane. Several famous Presbyterian ministers have also come from the FINLEY line. But, alongside with the pride taken in their religion, the tragic side of the FINLEYs' religious struggles must be examined.

In the Handbook of Denominations in the United States, a commentary on the influence John CALVIN had upon Presbyterianism says, "He gave courage to British Presbyterians in their bitter struggle against Catholic Bloody Mary. To him came Scots who became Covenanters; to him came John Knox, who went home to cry, `Great God, give me Scotland, or I die.' Knox and the Covenanters set Scotland afire and made it Protestant and Presbyterian."

John FOX, who lived in England from 1517 to 1587, gave graphic accounts in his Book of Martyrs of several Protestants who were burnt at the stake in Scotland in the 1500s. One of the first martyrs was said to be Patrick HAMILTON, who became acquainted with Martin LUTHER and professed his doctrines, much to the disapproval of the Catholic Bishop of St. Andrew's. His crimes were said to be "publicly disapproving of pilgramages, purgatory, prayers to saints, for the dead, etc." FOX describes his torture as follows:

"When he arrived at the stake, he kneeled down, and for some time prayed with great fervency. After this, he was fastened to the stake, and the fagots placed round him. A quantity of gunpowder, having been placed under his arms, was first set on fire, which scorched his left hand and one side of his face, but did no material injury, neither did it communicate with the fagots.

"In consequence of this, more powder and combustible matter were brought, which being set on fire, took effect, and the fagots being kindled, he called out, with an audible voice: `Lord Jesus, receive my spirit! How long shall darkness overwhelm this realm? And how long wilt thou suffer the tyranny of these men?'

"The fire, burning slow, put him to great torment, but he bore it with Christian magnanimity. What gave him the greatest pain was the clamor of some wicked men set on by the friars, who frequently cried, 'Turn, thou heretic; call upon our Lady; say, Salve Regina, etc.'

"To whom he replied, 'Depart from me, and trouble me not, ye messengers of Satan.' To one CAMPBELL, a friar, who was the ringleader, continuing to interrupt him by opprobrious language, said to him, 'Wicked man, God forgive thee.' After which, being prevented from futher speech by the violence of the smoke, and the rapidity of the flames, he resigned up his soul into the hands of Him who gave it. This steadfast believer in Christ suffered martyrdom in the year 1527."

I point out the above to set the context in which STOUT, in The Clan Finley, Vol. 1, First Edition (1940), says, "One Rev. John FINLEY, the last martyr to Christ's Crown and Covenant, was burned at the stake in Edinburgh just prior to the expulsion of James II."

Charles A. HANNA, in The Scotch-Irish Families in America, Vol. 2, Appendix R, p. 237, confirms this fact, as he includes an account of the confession of the Rev. John FINLAY of Kilmarnock, which he says is taken from a book published in 1714, A Cloud of Witnesses.

The account states that John FINLAY lived in Muirside, Kilmarnock Parish, and suffered in the Grass-market of Edinburgh on 15 Dec 1682. By giving his lengthy testimony, he states to his oppressors that he is "Shewing you that I am condemned unjustly by a generation of bloody men, who is thirsting after the blood of the saints of God, and upon no other account, but for my being found in the way of my duty in the sight of God; glory to his holy name for it, though gone about with many failings, much imperfections, for adhering to Christ and all his offices, as Prophet, Priest and King; and for my following him in all his persecuted gospel truths."

During this same period in our history, the first of the FINLEYs migrated to America. It is certain that in view of such persecution, one of the reasons for the exodus from Scotland was the degree of religious tolerance allowed in the New World.

Part 7: Last of the True Scotch-Irish

From all available records, it appears the first FINLEYs in America reached the New World in the mid- to late 1600s. As we saw above, there were martyrs among our ancestors in Scotland and they had very good reasons to leave the homeland in which they had been a vital part of its history. However, there were some FINLEYs who were able to amass some land holdings throughout the 1600s in Scotland and Ireland, and it is evident that not all FINLEYs came to America, as some of these holdings were passed on to other relatives.

John FINLEY, who was baptized 8 June 1579, St. Andrew's Parish, County Fife, Scotland; d 6 Oct 1670, Incharvie, County Fife; m (1st) Eleanor FORBES; m (2nd) 3 Oct 1630, Sarah CRAIGIE, d 1669; and he appeared in different leases up to 1668.

According to FRANCE, Buren's Book of Commoners," P. 229, shows baptisms of St. Andrew's Church, including John and Sarah CRAIGIE's children.

Their first son, James, was baptized 9 Sept 1631, St. Andrew's Parish, County Fife; d 16 Feb 1681, Incharvie, County Fife. On 14 July 1670, he was served as heir to his father.

In a Scotch Deed, James FINLEY, partitioner of Incharvie, County Fife, has a grantor's bond dated 22 June 1652 and 10 Aug 1670. Margaret MACKIE, spouse of James FINLEY, partitioner, has a grantor's bond dated 1 Aug 1669 and 18 Jan 1670. STOUT says James FINLEY was granted land in 1652 in Newburn Parish, Balchrystie, County Fife, Scotland, and appears in Newburn Parish records up to 1679.

james FINLEY m (1st) 1649 Barbara HENDERSON, who d 1665 (WOOD's date; STOUT says 1658), with no issue; m (2nd) 10 Sept 1666, Margaret MACKIE (WOOD says MOCKIE; TORRENCE says MC KAY; FRANCE says MCKIE), daughter of Alexander MACKIE. She d 1672 with a will dated June 1672.

The second son of John and Sarah CRAIGIE was my direct ancestor, Robert FINLEY, baptised 4 May 1634, Incharvie, County Fife, Scotland; d 18 June

1712, Mullaghabrac Parish, County Armagh, Ireland; m 1680, Mullaghabrac Parish, County Armagh, Ireland, w Margaret LAUDER, daughter of Julian LAUDER of Kellyreiadin, County Armagh.

FRANCE, TORRENCE and STOUT give much information on this family. Although Robert FINLEY was born in Incharvie, County Fife, Scotland, records show he sold his lands there to his cousin, Thomas FINLEY (son of James and Barbara HUNTAR FINLEY) about 1678, or the date on which he went to Ireland. STOUT says Robert FINLEY graduated from the University of Glasgow, Scotland, in 1658.

He first settled in Hamilton Bann and later went to Mogharunter, Parish Mullaghabrac. FRANCE and STOUT say in Deed Book 187 (TORRENCE says Irish Deeds, Book 262), P. 42, is found: "Admor (administration) of the land and goods of Robert FINLEY, of the Parish of Mullaghabrac, County Armagh, Ireland, John FINLEY, lawful son of said deceased Robert FINLEY, July 20, 1712, for the sole use of said Michael, Robert, Samuel, Archibald and John FINLEY, children of the said deceased."

In Irish Deeds, Book 262, P. 630, is found: "A memorial of deeds of lease and release, dated the 16th and 17th of January 1732, Robert, Samuel and John FINLEY, of the Parish of Mullaghabrac, Armagh, of the one part, and Michael FINLEY, of the said Parish, of the other part, reciting that the said Robert, Samuel and John, in consideration of Pounds 50, did convey to the said Michael, land and buildings in the said parish and county, bounded on the south by a house, then in possession of said Michael, to hold during the lives of the said Robert, Samuel and John, with proviso for redemption."

The baptismal records of Robert FINLEY's children are inscribed in the Parish Register in Mallaghabrac, County Armagh, Ireland. More on this line will appear in a minute, but first, let's go back to the children of James and Margaret MACKIE FINLEY:

Alexander FINLEY was baptized at St. Andrew's Church, County Fife, Scotland, on 30 July 1667; d 28 Jan 1736, Dublin, Ireland; m 10 Jan 1687, County Derry, Ireland, w Margaret JENNINGS, b 1668, d 1742, Dublin,

Ireland, daughter of William and Margaret MORDUCK JENNINGS. In 1688, he became a freeman by birth and then in 1690, he fought in King William's War. He was a woolen merchant in Dublin from 1691 to 1736. Records published by the Dublin Parish Society, St. Peter's Church, Dublin, Ireland, include Alexander FINLEY, buried 28 Jan 1736; Chancery Bill, Dublin, dated 12 May 1736; letters of administration granted Margaret FINLEY, relict of Alexander FINLEY, deceased, merchant of Little Green Street (the latter gives names of heirs; more on this line will follow).

The second child of James and Margaret MACKIE FINLEY was Margaret FINLEY, baptized 8 Aug 1668. No other information is available on her.

The next child was James FINLEY JR., baptized 10 June 1670; d 1738, Incharvie; m 14 June 1693 (STOUT incorrectly says 10 Oct 1693), St. Andrew's Church, Glasgow, Scotland, w Isabella INGLIS. He was a farmer at Paisley, Scotland. Their children were Margaret, b 1694; Ann, b 1695; John, b 1696; Rachel, b 1697, d 1720; Andrew, b 1700; Isabella, b 1701; Robert, b 1704, d before 1744 in the Carolinas (on 8 Sept 1744, administration of his goods were granted to creditors, Thomas WILLY, merchant of London, and David CORREA, merchant of Glasgow, though plenty of assets); Alexander, b 1706; James, b 22 Aug 1708, Paisley, Scotland, d 1768, Glasgow, Scotland, m 26 June 1734, Ann MC DONALD (he was co-owner of wool firm of FINLEY and MC DONALD); and Richard, b 1709.

The fourth child was John FINLEY, baptized 11 Apr 1672; d 12 Sept 1758, Dublin, Ireland; m Elizabeth POWER, who was buried 8 Dec 1732. John and his brother, Alexander, moved from County Fife, Scotland, to County Derry, Ireland, prior to 1687. John FINLEY also served in King William's War. Upon restoration of peace, he was engaged in the woolen trade.

The children of Alexander and Margaret JENNINGS FINLEY appear in the baptismal records of St. Peter's Church, Dublin. It is through them that the way to the New World was paved:

James FINLEY was baptized in St. Peter's Church, Dublin, Ireland on 4 Dec 1687; d 10 Feb 1753, Cumberland County, PA; m 10 Jan 1706, St. Peter's

Church, Dublin, w Elizabeth PATTERSON, b 1690, d 1755, daughter of Robert and Margaret FULLERTON PATTERSON.

Samuel FINLEY was baptized 10 Oct 1689; d 1751, West Nottingham Township, Cecil County, MD; m 10 May 1709, St. Andrew's Church (STOUT says St. Audon's), Dublin, w Jean WHYTE.

John FINLEY was baptized 23 Aug 1691; d before 1764, Shrewsbury Township, York County, PA; m 9 Feb 1711, St. Andrew's Church, Dublin, Ireland, w Eliza Marie MC NEALE (STOUT incorrectly lists his marriage to Alice MITCHELL on 18 Feb 1711. However, TORRENCE says that John FINLEY was the grandson of James and Barbara HUNTAR FINLEY).

William FINLEY was baptized 6 May 1694; d 1772, Ardstraw, County Tyrone, Ireland; m Agnes (last name unknown). He came to America but returned to Ireland.

Alexander FINLEY JR. was baptized 10 March 1696; d 25 Feb 1774, Dublin, Ireland; m Mary (STOUT says Jean) PATTERSON.

Margaret FINLEY was baptized 20 May 1697; m 28 Jan 1716, St. Peter's Church, Dublin, w Thomas PARNHAM.

In Dublin Deed Book 221, on 18 Jan 1720, James FINLEY gives a letter of attorney to his brother, Alexander FINLEY. In March 1720, there is an action of James FINLEY vs. Alexander FINLEY, elder, concerning a house on George Lane. There is a memorial of surrender of lease dated 16 March 1720 between James FINLEY and Alexander FINLEY JR., whereby, for certain consideration, the said James FINLEY did surrender a house on Cornmarket Street. Both John and Samuel FINLEY gave power of attorney to their brother, Alexander.

WOOD says James FINLEY, his wife and seven sons (STOUT lists nine sons); Samuel FINLEY, his wife and five sons; and John FINLEY, his wife and six children, all immigrated to America on the ship, Eagle Wing, landing at Newcastle, DE, on 22 May 1720.

STOUT adds the following information: "Maryland and Pennsylvania because of their guarantee of religious freedom were attractive to the Celts and to these colonies, the tide of Scotch-Irish immigration quickly turned. To the rising effects of this immigration many ships were built for the purpose of carrying passengers and goods to America.

"Among the ships built for this purpose was the brig Eagle Wing, launched at Belfast, Ireland, in the year 1714 and in constant service for more than 35 years between that port and the ports of Newcastle, DE, or Philadelphia. It was a fast-sailing vessel, modern for the times, making the trip to America, if all went well, in seven to 10 weeks.

"This ship is of importance in our history since so many of the Clan were numbered among its passengers on its many voyages to our shores. It is a tradition, likely, though without documentary proof, that on several voyages the Scots chartered the brig in order to obtain thereby reduced wares. Even in those days, our ancestors were given to being cautious with their cash."

James and Elizabeth PATTERSON's first son, John, m Thankful DOAK. This line leads to Polly FINLEY, who m Davy CROCKETT. Carmen FINLEY has commented on one of John and Thankful DOAK's children, William Joseph, and that information will be presented later. But, for now, let's return to the children of Robert and Margaret LAUDER FINLEY:

Robert FINLEY JR. was baptized 9 May 1681, Mullaghabrac, County Armagh, Ireland; d 1741, West Nottingham Township, Chester County, PA; m 2 Aug 1718, Ireland, w Sarah PATTERSON, daughter of John PATTERSON. His will was dated 10 Oct 1739, proved 20 July 1741 and filed 30 Nov 1742. Robert and Sarah PATTERSON FINLEY's children were Mary, b 1719, m John JOHNSTONE; and Robert FINLEY III, baptized 11 Feb 1720, County Antrim, Ireland, d 21 April 1808, Rising Sun, Cecil County, MD, m Frances BOYD. The family moved from Ireland to America in 1732 and settled in Chester County, PA.

Michael FINLEY was b 10 Feb 1683; baptized 7 May 1683, Mullaghabrac, County Armagh, Ireland; d 1750, Salisbury Township, Chester County, PA; m

12 July 1712, Ireland, by the Rev. George Hall w Ann O'NEILL, daughter of Samuel O'NEILL. Michael FINLEY and his family, and his brother, Archibald FINLEY, and his family, immigrated on the Eagle Wing, arriving in Philadelphia, PA on 28 Sept 1734.

Michael FINLEY first settled in Bucks County, PA, and then to Salisbury Township, Chester County, PA, where his name and that of Michael FINLEY JR. appear on the 1747 tax list. Michael and Ann O'NEILL FINLEY were the ancestors of the Rev. Samuel FINLEY, president of the College of New Jersey (now Princeton University); Henry Agard WALLACE, Vice President of the United States under Franklin Delano Roosevelt; the Colgate family; Samuel Finley Breese MORSE, inventor of the telegraph; and Major Albert Finley FRANCE.

Samuel FINLEY was baptized 4 May 1684; d 1737, West Nottingham Township, MD. He immigrated in 1732 and died unmarried.

Archibald FINLEY was baptized on 8 Jan 1686; d 11 March 1752, New Britain Township, Bucks County, PA; m 10 Aug 1721, Ireland, Margaret KELSO, daughter of Henry KELSO. They immigrated in 1734.

John FINLEY was baptized on 14 June 1688; d 9 Dec 1760, Hopewell Township, York County, PA; m 22 Nov 1714, Ireland, w Mary Ann BARCLAY. They immigrated in 1732 and first settled in Nottingham Township, then moved to Chester County, where they lived from 1739 to 1744. He was an elder in Rock Presbyterian Church, organized in 1714. Prior to 1751, John FINLEY and two of his sons, Andrew and John JR., moved to Hopewell Township and on 1 Apr 1751, John FINLEY SR. received a warrant for 50 acres of land and on 4 Apr 1754, received a warrant for 100 acres. He became a member of Donegal Presbyterian Church and helped to organize the Lower Chanceford Presbyterian Church in 1757. His son, John JR., was a trustee. His wife, Mary Ann BARCLAY, was baptized 6 May 1692, Glenarn Parish, County Antrim, Ireland; d before 1760, Hopewell Township, PA. She was the daughter of James and Mary STEEL BARCLAY and the granddaughter of John and Mary CAMPBELL BARCLAY.

The Finleys of Bucks, written by Warren S. ELY on 5 Mar 1902, gives a fairly complete history of Archibald FINLEY's family, as follows:

"Archibald FINLEY, Archibald KELSO, Thomas KELSO and Henry KELSO contracted with George FITZWATER about the year 1736 for a tract of 500 acres of land in New Britain Township, Bucks County, lying along the Northwest side of the present Upper State Road and extending from the Bristol Road 550 perches toward the county line.

"George FITZWATER died before any conveyance in fee was executed and directors his executors to convey when the balance of the purchase money was paid. By mutual agreement, this tract was partitioned between the parties above mentioned and the part allotted to Archibald FINLEY was 151 acres and 53 perches off the end toward the county line, adjoining John FOREMAN, the greater part of which was recently the property of Elias SELLERS.

"Archibald FINLEY died in a house he had erected on this tract on March 11, 1749-50 and the deed therefore was made by the executors of George FITZWATER on December 11, 1750 to his widow, Margaret FINLEY, and his two eldest sons, John and Henry FINLEY, as the executors of Archibald FINLEY, deceased.

"The will of Archibald FINLEY was a nuncupative one and is as follows: Memorandum that on the Eleventh day of March Anno Domini 1749-50, Archibald FINLEY of New Britain in the County of Bucks and Province of Pennsylvania, Mason, being very sick in body but of sound mind and memory (to all appearances) Did Declare as his last will and Testament That it was his will that his wife, Margaret FINLEY, and his two eldest sons (that is) John FINLEY and Henry FINLEY, should be his executors and that all his Estate shall be divided and distributed amongst his wife and children as the Law Directs in case of Intestates Estates.

"And further that he named and Appointed Simon BUTLER of New Britain, aforesaid Esqr., and Isaac JAMES of Montgomery in the County of Philadelphia to be Trustees to See and take Care that not any of his children should be wronged, Which verbal Will the above said Archibald FINLEY made and published in the hearing of us the under subscribers. As witness our hands this Twelveth Day of March A.D. 1749-50. Robert LALOR, Henry KELSO, James FINLEY.

"This will was proven on March 27, 1750 by the above witnesses who state in their affidavits that FINLEY died soon after making the declaration and that the declaration was reduced to writing after his death. Letters testamentary were issued to the widow, Margaret FINLEY, and the eldest son, John. The Inventory of the Goods and Chattels of Archibald FINLEY, deceased, was made by Benjamin SNODGRASS and Hugh BARKLEY on March 23, 1749-50.

"Archibald FINLEY left to survive him at least two other sons, Alexander FINLEY, and Archibald FINLEY (JR.), and a daughter, Agnes, wife of Henry KELSO.

"Alexander FINLEY purchased on January 1, 1749-50, a tract of 78 acres on the opposite side of the State Road from that of his father, now in the township of Warrington, the present Whitehall Turnpike being its eastern boundary. The farm was late the property of Nathan HOUPT. Alexander FINLEY died on this farm in 1779, leaving a widow, Mary, an only son, James, who died on the same farm in 1836, and daughters, Jane, Mary, Martha and Sarah.

"Archibald FINLEY JR. became the landlord of the old hotel at the present borough of Chalfont in 1763, succeeding Arthur THOMAS who had been there since 1751. FINLEY was succeeded by Nicholas KOOKER in 1765, though FINLEY again obtained the license in 1766. This is the latest record we have of Archibald FINLEY and he probably removed with the rest of the family to Loudon County, Virginia at about this date.

"Henry FINLEY, the second son of Archibald, married Elizabeth, daughter of William WALKER, who owned several large tracts of land in Warrington, lying along the county line and the Lower State Road. He joined in the conveyance of the paternal acres in 1752. In 1758, he was living in Hilltown Township at the present site of Dublin as shown by a petition to the Court of Quarter Sessions in June of that year. He soon removed with his family to Loudon County, Virginia, and from there into Kentucky in 1788 as recited in the American Ararat.' Little is known of his family except that one of his daughters married Lieut. John WALLACE, who removed with his family to Kentucky."

One thing which should be noted in the above section (which came from a publication of the Bucks County Historical Society, Doylestown, PA) are the dual dates. In "Tracing Your Ancestry," by HELMBOLD, as quoted in the Ashley County, AR Genealogical Society's Spring 1988 issue of "Kin Kollecting": "In 1752, the Julian calendar was supplanted by the Georgian calendar. However, the other change made at that time is a little more difficult to perceive. Because of differing customs among the settlers, the new year began on 25 March or on 1 January. When the calendar was changed, the Parliament also established 1 January 1752 as the legal New Year's Day.

"Birthdays of people then had to be expressed as old style or new style. For example, a date would be written as 14 February 1727/8. This means that the event took place in 1727 if the year was thought to begin on 25 March, but the birthdate was in 1728 if the year was thought to begin on 1 January. Since the 25 March date is the turning point, only dates from 1 January to 24 March have to be indicated in the above way."

Part 8: John Findley, The Pathfinder

51

In a footnote to ELY's previous narrative, he states, "The memory of John FINDLEY (so spelled by DRAPER), the precursor and pilot of BOONE to Kentucky, merits a brighter page on Western history than the meagre facts will warrant. Of all the pioneers,' exclaims Ex-Governor Morehead in his Boonesborough address, the least justice has been done to FINLEY.'" The manuscripts of Lyman C. DRAPER, referred to above, reportedly have a wealth of information about John FINDLEY as well as others in our family. They are contained at the Wisconsin Historical Society, as well as at the LDS Library in Salt Lake City. I will give a complete list of the manuscripts' call letters at the end of this section.

DRAPER says that autographs show the spelling of the name as John FINDLEY. Although others use different spellings, the spelling has been changed in this report to reflect DRAPER's account. FRANCE, STOUT and TORRENCE, as well as others, agree that John FINDLEY was the son of Archibald and Margaret KELSO FINLEY, b 27 June 1722, County Armagh, Ireland; m 15 Sept 1744, Paxtang Township, PA, w Elizabeth HARRIS, b 1 June 1720; d 7 Aug 1769, Harris Ferry, PA.

Their first child was Esther FINLEY, b 22 Aug 1745, Paxtang Township, Lancaster County, PA; d 1789. She m Col. William PATTERSON, b ca. 1737, Lancaster County, PA. According to TORRENCE, he had married first Isabella GALBRAITH, b 1744; d 29 Oct 1764, daughter of Capt. John and Dorcas SMITH GALBRAITH. PATTERSON was the son of James and Mary STUART PATTERSON, whose place on the Susquehanna River was known as "Liberty Hall." Col. William and Esther FINLEY PATTERSON had five children: John PATTERSON, b 1767, m Sarah RAY; Isabella PATTERSON, m David HUNTER; William Augustus PATTERSON, b 17 Apr 1772, m Hannah Maria SPENCE; Margaret PATTERSON, died young; and James PATTERSON, b 1776.

The second child of John and Elizabeth HARRIS FINLEY was Martha Finley, b 3 Jun 1747; m William WERTZ. Their children were John Finley WERTZ, b 1768; Isabella WERTZ, b 1770; Martha WERTZ, b 1771; William WERTZ JR., b 1772; and Jane WERTZ.

The third child was John FINLEY JR., b 28 Sept 1760, Salisbury, Lancaster County, PA; d 11 Mar 1846, near St. Charles, Kane County, IL. He m (1st) 14 Sept 1780, Washington County, PA, w Priscilla HAYS, b 1761; d 4 Feb 1845, near Hardinsburg, Dearborn County, IN. Their children were David FINLEY, b 10 Dec 1781, probably Washington County, PA (birthplace also reported as KY); d 29 Aug 1853, near Danville, Vermillion County, IL; m 1803, Nancy MILLER; and Priscilla FINLEY, b 2 Nov 1783, probably Washington County, PA, d 1803, probably Dearborn County, IN. She is reported to have died from smallpox; also was reported to have gone by the name of MILLER (her mother's second husband). Priscilla HAYS FINLEY separated from John FINLEY JR. when he showed the tendency of his father to wander. She then m (2nd) Thomas MILLER.

John FINLEY JR. m (2nd) 28 Jul 1796, Ohio County, VA (now WV), w Sarah MOORE, b 20 Oct 1765, York County, PA; d 27 May 1823, Delaware County, OH. (It is through this marriage that my line continues. It should be noted that STOUT is incorrect on P. 107, Vol. I, Second Edition of "The Clan Finley," where he lists John FINLEY (5-02-151) as m (2nd) Sarah MOORE. That John FINLEY is shown as m (1st) Elizabeth ANDERSON.)

Their first child was David F. FINLEY, b 6 Feb 1798, Brooke County, VA (now WV); d 26 Nov 1872, DeKalb County, IL; m 24 Dec 1828, Delaware County, OH, w Mary LOWRIE, b 28 Jul 1796, Ireland; d 9 Mar 1856, DeKalb County, IL; both buried in Ohio Grove Cemetery.

The second child was Agnes (Nancy) FINLEY, b 12 Feb 1800, Brooke County, VA (now WV); d 10 Dec 1830, Delaware County, OH; m 12 Feb 1824, Delaware County, OH, w Joseph HARTER, b 4 May 1799; d 19 May 1831; both buried Oak Grove Cemetery.

My ancestor was the third child, Robert FINLEY, b 12 Nov 1801, Brooke County, VA (now WV); d 17 May 1877, Kane County, IL; m 1829, Delaware County, OH, w Elizabeth RILEY, b 1807, PA; d 19 Jul 1875, Kane County, IL; both buried in Garfield Cemetery.

The next child was Sally (Sarah) FINLEY, b 17 Dec 1804, Jefferson County, OH; d 1872; m probably Delaware County, OH, w John B. LEONARD. The last child was Jane FINLEY, b 27 Aug 1807, Jefferson County, OH; d 11 Mar 1840, near Kilbourne, Delaware County, OH; m probably Delaware County, OH, w Isaac LEONARD, b 7 Jul 1807; d 3 Oct 1844, Delaware County, OH; both buried Old Kilbourne Cemetery, OH; he m (2nd) Nancy THURSTON.

Most of the above information about the family of John FINLEY JR. comes from Rex Bird FINLEY and Mary Louise ALCORN. ALCORN, 2818 119th St., Toledo, OH 43611, although not yet a subscriber, wrote a paper about the ancestors of Sarah MOORE. In this paper, she quotes from the pension papers of John FINLEY JR., who appeared in the Delaware County, OH Court of Common Pleas on 21 Apr 1834, but who was denied a pension because he was unable to provide sufficient proof of his length of service on the Pennsylvania Line from Washington County during the Revolutionary War.

However, in going back to John FINDLEY, the Pathfinder, an extraordinary record of service to the fledging nation is found. According to FRANCE, he grew up in the log cabin that his father, Archibald FINLEY, built.

FRANCE says, "The education of young FINDLEY was necessarily very defective. There were no schools then established in this remote district of log cabins. Thus reared up in the frontier of Pennsylvania, a woodsman and hunter by nature and habits, he was man of strong marked character, shunning the dense settlements and preferring to rove in the solitary wilderness.

"Keen habits of observation, an expert marksman, he soon profited in the pursuit of game which led him on long hunting trips, from which he would return ladened with furs and skins. He became inured to hardship and endurance and to rely on his own resources, with great bodily vigor and to be the first man to appreciate the fertile lands of Kentucky; the first Anglo-Saxon to build a cabin on them and who later was to pilot Daniel BOONE.

"In appearance (from military record) John FINDLEY was well set; five feet, six inches in height; broad shoulders and deep chest with dark complexion; dark hair and blue eyes. FILSON says, He was not a man to get soured by misfortune, for he looked kindlier on the bright side of life rather than on the dark side of things.

"In the year of 1744 at the age of 22, John FINDLEY had received from the Colony of Pennsylvania a license as Indian Trader; he received licenses in 1745, 1746, 1748, but not in 1747, the year in which he was granted land in Paxtang Township. It may be that he spent that year in hewing out his farm and installing his young wife and their growing family in the home.

"He had become associated with John HARRIS, who was one of the oldest and most active traders on the Susquehanna. HARRIS' settlement was just above the mouth of Paxtang Creek, which during the settlement of Cumberland Valley by the Scotch-Irish, became a place of importance, and here a ferry was established, called, Harris Ferry, on the site where Harrisburg, PA now stands.

"John FINDLEY soon fell in love with Elizabeth, oldest daughter of John HARRIS (JR.) and his wife, Esther SAY, and they were married on Sept. 15, 1744 by Rev. John Elder of the Paxtang Presbyterian Church.

"John FINDLEY made raiding trips from Harris Ferry as far west as the present state of Ohio and in time became a famous Indian trader, frontiersman and Indian fighter, experiencing many perils and adventures in his rambles. In 1748 John FINDLEY was trading as far west as the Allegheny, toward which stream the Eastern Indians had been drifting since 1730. He had made his headquarters at Shanopinstown, a small trading post at the site where Pittsburgh now stands.

(In The History Quarterly, published at the University of Louisville, KY in April 1927, sent to me by Ron ROSSI, Lucien BECKNER writes, "Thomas CRESAP, Virginia's agent in the Ohio territory, wrote Governor Dinwiddie in 1751 that one James FINDLEY and another are suspected to be taken and carried off by the French, who make a practice of carrying off our men every year; therefore, I think it highly necessary to take the French that are at Logstown and detain them till those of ours taken last year, as well as those suspected to be taken this year, are restored.' The above James' is our John, and Logstown was a post located a few miles below the present Pittsburgh.")

"We find his name as a witness together with Hugh CRAWFORD, John GRAY, David HENDRICKS and Aaron PRICE to the letter which the Indians sent to the Governor of Pennsylvania.

"In the spring of 1752, FINDLEY, Paul PRICE and William BRYAN were partners in a trading post at Peckawellany, the big Pect-town near the present city of Piqua, Ohio. According to an affidavit made by William BRYAN four years later, the goods were valued at 1,142 pounds. In an attack on this town, where English settlers were being harbored, the French confiscated or destroyed these goods. Whether FINDLEY was here at the time does not appear. After this occurence, being discouraged by his losses, he returned to his home in Paxtang.

"John FINDLEY was now 30 years old. No doubt learning much from the Indians, he described the Ohio River far away in the West, pouring its flood into the impenetrable forest; the amount of game to be found in those realms. By pointing to the leaf of the forests and of an Indian village, the voyage in a canoe, in the language of the Indian, required two paddles, two warriors and three moons.

"With a fortune swept away, and still undaunted, he bought another stock of goods, and with four assistants, he crossed the mountains of the Alleghenies, as far as the Indian village of Logstown and in a canoe, descended the Ohio River as far down as the falls of the Ohio, where now stands the city of Louisville, Kentucky. He met a company of Shawnees at the mouth of Big Bone Creek. These Indians were going to take their fall and winter hunt in the interior of Kentucky, where they assured FINDLEY he would find a rich harvest of furs and skins, promising to assist in the transportation of his cargo of goods and to trade with him as fast as they could obtain pelts. A hatchet, a knife, a string of beads and trinkets that could be bought for a small sum could be exchanged in the wigwam of the Indians for furs and skins of priceless value and sold to foreign shippers at a great profit.

"To this invitation, FINDLEY consented to join the party from Big Bone Creek, along the Indian path through the beautiful valley of Kentucky. They arrived at an Indian village, situated on the Lulbegrud Creek between the

Licking and Kentucky River, located in Clark County, about 11 miles from Winchester, KY and called by the Indians by the uncouth name of Eskeppaki, meaning, Old Corn Fields.' Here, FINDLEY erected a cabin and surrounded it with a stockade. Displaying his gaudy wares to the admiring eyes of the Indian, he soon started a brisk trade and while he was busy gathering furs and skins, other traders from Pennsylvania encamped close by. From these traders and the Indians, he first learned of the great Warriors Path, which ran south to Cumberland Gap. It was this memory of this gateway, from his old cabin on Lulbegrud Creek, that 16 years later helped to fire Daniel BOONE to make his expedition to Kentucky in 1769.

"After awhile, disputes arose between the traders and a party of outlaws, Conewagoes and French Indians, in which several of the traders were made prisoners and three of FINDLEY's men were killed. This occurred on April 10, 1753, but John FINDLEY and John FALKNER made their escape.

(TORRENCE notes that FINDLEY served as a scout under George CROGHAN in 1754; DRAPER, quoted by ELY, says, "FINDLEY was probably one of the party who, under George CROGHAN, had tendered their services to BRADDOCK and were received in a cold, indifferent manner.)

"July 9, 1755 was memorable in the history of the West. General BRADDOCK, fresh from England, had arrived on the Potomac with a large Regular Army. He set out to teach the Frenchmen a lesson. So, on March 10, with 86 officers and 1,373 men, he reached Wills Creek, where WASHINGTON, with some hundred Colonial Militia had been at work during the preceding winter and had built Fort Cumberland.

"With BRADDOCK's army were 100 hardy frontiersmen under Captain Edward B. DOBBS and with him was Daniel BOONE. Here, also, came George CROGHAN and his men and among them was John FINDLEY. Under what circumstances FINDLEY and BOONE met, we do not know. Over the campfire, amidst the din and clangor of war, FINDLEY found in the hardy North Caroliniana frontiersman a kindred spirit. Fascinated, BOONE absorbed the tales of this Scotch-Irishman, his recitals of his explorations of that country called Kentucky, the ideal hunter's paradise, richness of soil and abundance of game. BOONE was possessed with the desire to gaze with his own eyes on this wonderful land. Both of them were young and neither of them realized in the light of the campfire that they were making history of worldwide interest.

"BOONE had been assigned to the duties of a wagoneer and mechanic on the strength of his blacksmithing experiences. The wagon train was the center of a fierce attack of the howling Indians. Troops of BRADDOCK staggered under the cruel fire. They seemed to be confused by the fiendish clamor and the invisibility of the foe. ST. CLAIR's working force came up on a run, to pile confusion on confusion and the head of the column was speedily wiped out. Then BRADDOCK's mechanical discipline began to give ground before the marksmanship of the enemy. With the ancient forest hemming in the road with no visible foe, the army was as helpless as a blind man.

"The best-equipped and proudest army that England had ever sent over to North America was a rabble of crazy men. The Virginian fighting from tree to tree, behind a barricade of a fallen tree, soon cleared the side of the road and drove the savages from the terrible ravine. When BRADDOCK ordered the retreat, only a third of the army was left. Once the retreat was sounded, those who could walk, began an insane rush to reach the river.

"Colonel WASHINGTON now had all the riflemen fighting in Indian fashion and on this manuever, saved them from being annihilated, as 450 officers and men were slain outright. What BOONE and FINDLEY were doing all this time, history does not tell us. Being expert riflemen, they no doubt were doing their share of fighting, side by side, and in the retreat on the backs of wagon horses, they arrived safely at Wills Creek.

"The whereabouts of John FINDLEY for the next two years is lost to history. As war had put an end to his trade, he doubtless spent these years in becoming better acquainted with his family and protecting his home from the savages. The next we hear of him is a record in the Pennsylvania Archives, Sixth Series, Vol. 1, where on May 9, 1759, age 36 years, he had enlisted as a Scout in a regiment under Captain Charles MC CLUNG to protect the frontier from the Indians. After the French had been driven out of Fort Duquesne, it was renamed Fort Pitt. In the census of Fort Pitt, July 1760, we find John FINDLEY and 80 Pennsylvania traders had settled there.

"In 1763, he was with Colonel BOUQUET as interpreter, understanding the Indian language, in his fight with the Indians at Turtle Creek. Under date of March 9, 1766, he commanded a batteau called The Otto' with a cargo of goods for Fort Chartres. (BECKNER writes that this was part of a fleet of five boats from the Philadelphia trading house of Baynton, Wharton and Morgan, and that the fleet reached the fort around April 1. On the way down, "The Otto" had trouble and had to be lightened.) He returned to Lancaster County and outfitted a new business (horse trading), as he was in the Yadkin Valley, North Carolina late in 1768.

"Daniel BOONE, from his home in North Carolina, made long excursions in western Carolina and Tennessee, but it was his secret ambition to scale the mountain or through the Cumberland Gateway to the mysterious country, Kentucky. During the winter of 1768 to 1769, Daniel BOONE was agreeably surprised by the arrival of his old comrade-in-arms, and throughout the winter, John FINDLEY was Boone's guest. During that cold winter, uppermost in the minds of both was the thought of the new country that FINDLEY had explored.

(BECKNER adds, "Judge Moses BOONE, a son of Squire BOONE, in a statement to Dr. DRAPER, told how FINDLEY used to leave his spare horses with the BOONEs while he went out to trade; and how upon his return, he sat around the fire and told about the wonder-place, Kentucky, where he had traded with the Indians.")

"To them, there were no hardships in the journey and the idea of a journey of a few hundred miles in the wilderness was not one to be regarded by them with any special solicitude. Daniel BOONE soon formed a plan for organizing a small party for the expedition with his friend, Judge HENDERSON, who was head of a land company and by whom BOONE was encouraged to make the expedition as confidential agent for the land company.

"On May 1, 1769, a date memorial in the annals of American exploration, this company of rugged backwoodsmen, Daniel BOONE, John STUART, Joseph HOLDEN, James MOONEY and William COOLEY, under John FINDLEY's guidance, left their home on the Upper Yadkin and began that historical journey into the unknown country; each man fully equipped in the deerskin costume of that period, mounted on a good horse and leading a pack horse with a stock of provisions, blankets and bearskins, traps, rifles and ammunition, started on the long journey into the wilderness.

"Proceeding over Stone Mountain, through the valley of the Holston, over Iron Mountain, they passed through the Clinch across the Walden's Ridge, crossing rivers and dense forests. They came to Powell Valley, which at that time, was the farthest settlement of white men. Here, they found a hunters' trail, which led them to Cumberland Gap. They soon came to the Warriors Path, trodden by the Indians for generations. Following this for many miles, a fatiguing journey, which took them a full month, they at last reached what is now called Station Camp Creek, a tributary of the Kentucky River, in Estill County, so named because here was built their principal or Station Camp.

"In BOONE's account, DRAPER's manuscript, he said he and FINDLEY at once proceeded to take a more thorough survey of the country, and on 7 June 1769, we found ourselves on the Red River,' where John FINDLEY had formerly been trading with the Indians on Lulbegrud Creek, where nothing remained but charred embers of the Indian huts and part of the stockade built by FINDLEY still standing, which fully corroborated in his mind all that FINDLEY had related of Kentucky, and from the top of an eminence, they saw the beautiful level country of Kentucky. This was Pilot Knob, a few miles north of the present Clay City, Powell County. On Dec. 22, 1769, BOONE and John STUART set out on a hunting and exploring trip, when suddenly, a large party of Shawnees sprang from their concealment and seized them both as captives and forced STUART to lead them to their camp, where FINDLEY and the others were made prisoners.

"The Indians plundered the camp of everything it held: horses, furs, traps, rifles and ammunition. They were told they were trespassing on land which belonged to the red man, after which, to their infinite relief, they were released, given enough food to carry them back to the settlement and ordered to leave Kentucky at once. But BOONE and STUART infuriated at the idea of returning home poorer than they had left, and after a cautious pursuit, succeeded in entering the Shawnees' camp and made away with the horses. Two days later, the Shawnees having given chase, BOONE and STUART were captives once more.

"Meanwhile, FINDLEY, COOLEY, MOONEY and HOLDEN were homeward bound and after waiting several days, were convinced that BOONE and STUART had perished. At the same time, Squire BOONE and a hunter named NEILEY were hurrying westward, bringing horses and supplies, sent by the land company, and they were not far from Cumberland Gap. The two parties met and Squire learned from FINDLEY the news of the supposed death of BOONE and STUART. It was decided to return home. However, they had gone but a short way when they were halted by the sudden appearance of BOONE and STUART, who had succeeded in making their escape.

"Now, with fresh supplies, BOONE, STUART, Squire BOONE and NEILEY decided to remain longer. FINDLEY and the others decided that, for the present, they had enough of Kentucky and leaving these four men, started for home. Nothing happened to the homeward party and on reaching the Holston Valley, FINDLEY took the blazed trail through the frontier of Virginia, finally reaching his home in Lancaster County and found his wife had died 7 Aug 1769, while he was in Kentucky.

"In 1772, again the dauntless old trader fitted out for a trip into the wilderness, selling the Indians trinkets, for in a collection of newspaper records, under the date of June 3, 1772, is said: Several Senecas have been lately killed by our people and the Indians in revenge have murdered a whole family on Buffalo Creek and four families on the Youghighany and likewise killed Robert PARSONS and robbed John FINDLEY of about 500 pounds worth of goods.'

"After this loss, he must have returned to his home to try to raise another stake, as records of Cumberland County show a deed made by John FINDLEY, as acknowledged before William PATTERSON under date of Sept. 20, 1772 and signed by John FINDLEY, which speaks of Elizabeth, his late wife, formerly

Elizabeth HARRIS. It releases to John FINDLEY's daughter, Esther, wife of William PATTERSON, and to Margaret and John FINLEY JR., his life estate of land of 200 acres in Newberry Township and 162 acres in Paxtang Township. It is believed that John FINDLEY sought further adventure in Virginia in 1775, where he met Nicholas CRESWELL and gave CRESWELL, who was starting on an Indian trading expedition to Ohio, a letter of introduction and advice on the trade in Ohio.

"Whether he died alone, somewhere in the valley of the Ohio, or in the wilds of the West, tradition does not tell us."

Ron ROSSI, in notes along with BECKNER's article, states FINDLEY was wounded in a battle with Cherokees in 1776. Charles A. HANNA, in a letter to ELY, quotes John P. Hale's Trans-Allegheny Pioneers, P. 267, as saying, "John FINDLEY, the long-time frontiersman and wilderness pilot, being old and poor and wounded, asks Washington County, VA for aid in 1777." ELY also says HOWE's "Virginia" gives the court record under his account of Washington County, as follows, "At a Court continued and held for Washington County, February 26, 1777, John FINDLEY, making it appear to the satisfaction of the court of Washington County that he, upon the 20th day of July 1776, received a wound in the thigh in the battle fought with the Cherokees, near the Great Island (in Holston River, east Tennessee), and it now appears to said court that he, in consequence of said wound is unable to gain a living by his labor as formerly, therefore his case is recommended to the consideration of the General Assembly of the Commonwealth of Virginia."

Following the above, HANNA writes, "None of the above is inconsistent with the theory that John FINDLEY, the wilderness pilot, might have been the son of Archibald FINLEY."

In The Wilderness Trail, HANNA says, "In Mr. H. Addington BRUCE's recent book on Daniel BOONE and the Wilderness Road (N.Y., 1910), that writer states that one Stephen POMEROY, the first settler in what is now Huntsburg, Geauga County, Ohio, found living there in 1808, when he first went to that country, a trapper and trader named John FINDLEY, whose place of residence was on a stream still known as Finley Creek, and who told

POMEROY, according to the account of his great-grandson, that he had been with BOONE in Kentucky, and had fought under WAYNE. Mr. BRUCE states that this John FINDLEY enlisted in the War of 1812, returned to Huntsburg after the war, and, about 1818, removed, it was thought, to Maryland.

"As John FINDLEY, the trader who led BOONE into Kentucky, must have been born about 1720, it is scarcely probable that he could have been in active military service at the age of 90 or more, or that he was a trapper and trader at the age of 88 or thereabouts," comments DRAPER. So, the final resting place of John FINDLEY, the Pathfinder, remains a mystery even today.

However, Clark's Kentucky Almanac and Book of Facts 2006,claims, "FINLEY settled along the banks of the Licking River in 1796 and is buried not far from where he first settled (in Fleming County, KY)." I lived in West Kentucky for a while, but I have not been to Fleming County to confirm this. FRANCE acknowledges use of the works of HANNA, R.G. THWARTE, H.A. BRUCE, archives of various states, colonial records, Maryland Gazette, and Bible records of FINLEY and HARRIS families, plus the DRAPER manuscript narrative of Daniel BRYAN's notes of conversation with Moses and Isaiah BOONE by the Hon. Edward COLES, who visited Nathan BOONE in Missouri. DRAPER's very detailed account of the trip to Kentucky also appears in the chapter of "John FINDLEY and Kentucky Before BOONE," in Vol. II of HANNA's The Wilderness Trail.

Lyman C. Draper's Manuscripts

Lyman Copeland DRAPER was b 14 Sept 1815, New York; d 26 Aug 1891, WI. During his lifetime, he compiled about 50 series and/or sub-series of manuscripts relating to the history of KY, TN and VA. The originals are kept at the State Historical Society of Wisconsin, University of Wisconsin, 816 State St., Madison, WI 53706. The manuscripts are also available on microfilm from the LDS Library in Salt Lake City, UT. An index to Series CC, "Calendar of the Kentucky Papers of the DRAPER Collection of Manuscripts," is found on microfilm in the MISC Film Area, No. 0823866, Item 2. An index to Series XX and DD, "Calendar of the Tennessee and King's Mountain Papers of the

Draper Collections," is found in the U.S. and Canada Film Area, No. 0896963, Item 2.

Other films relating to our history are found in the U.S. and Canada Film Area, with film numbers in parentheses: Series B, Vol. 1-5, "Life of Daniel BOONE—1742-1799" (0889099); Series C, Vol. 4-6, "BOONE Manuscripts" (0889104); Series AA, Vol. 1-2, "IRVINE Papers" (John FINDLEY is in Vol. 1) (0889098); Series CC, Vol. 26-27, "Newspaper Extracts KY—1794-1849" (James FINDLEY is in Vol. 26) (0889119); Series E, Vol. 5-7, "BRADY and WETZEL" (Joseph L. FINLEY is in Vol. 5) (0889133); Series MM, Vol. 1-3, "PATTERSON" (Rev. Robert W. FINLEY is in Vol. 3) (0889177); Series NN, Vol. 1-5, "Pittsburgh and NW VA—1737-1814" (John FINDLEY is in Vol. 5) (0889179); Series U, Vol. 4-7, "Gen. Richard BUTLER, including War of 1812" (letters of Samuel FINLEY, possibly Gen. Samuel FINLEY of Mason County or Fleming County, KY) (0889206); and Series ZZ, Vol. 10-16, "Virginia" (John Evans FINLEY is in Vol. 12) (0889243).

Finley Marriage Records

I currently have almost 18,000 linked marriages stored on my genealogy data files. By linked marriages, I mean that each is linked onto a branch of the FINLEY family tree, with no loose ends. Some of the submitters have not found out yet where they tie in, but eventually, perhaps all FINLEYs can be joined together. In hopes that some links may be found, I am including the following lists of marriage records which have been sent to various archivals:

KENTUCKY: 1780-1900; Submitter: Virginia HANKS

17 May 1838, Fleming County: Andrew FINLEY w Sarah PLUMMER.

30 Dec 1833, Franklin County: Ann FINLEY w James HARDY.

2 Jan 1827, Fleming County: Betsy Ann FINLEY w Joseph B. FARIS.

31 Jan 1815, Lincoln County: Eliza FINLEY w William BAIRD.

22 Jan 1829, Hopkins County: Elizabeth FINLEY w Franklin M. NOEL.

17 Jan 1833, Hopkins County: George FINLEY w Elizabeth H. DOBYNS.

29 Jun 1786, Lincoln County: George FINLEY w Polly GAINES.

1 Oct 1795, Madison County: George FINLEY w Nancy HAGANS.

15 Aug 1812, Christian County: Hampton FINLEY w Nancy TAYLOR.

15 Oct 1839, Fleming County: Hannah S. FINLEY w Abiah DILLON.

11 Oct 1888, Knott County: Henrietta FINLEY w Peter ABLE.

8 Jul 1816, Hopkins County: Howard FINLEY w Nancy MOTT.

8 Jan 1819, Hardin County: Indianna FINLEY w Carter WRIGHT.

17 Nov 1848, Fleming County: James FINLEY w Maranda RICKETTS.

19 Oct 1808, Washington County: James C. FINLEY w Mary RAY.

2 Sept 1824, Adair County: James P. FINLEY w Charity WALBERT.

4 Feb 1814, Hopkins County: James FINLEY w Nancy DOBYNS.

13 May 1801, Garrard County: Jenny Ann FINLEY w Edmond SMITH.

29 Dec 1824, Hopkins County: Jesse M. FINLEY w Elizabeth JONES.

14 Sept 1809, Hardin County: John FINLEY w Polly BOZORTH.

23 Nov 1805, Christian County: John FINLEY w Hester CLARK.

5 Dec 1833, Fleming County: John FINLEY w Margaret DRENNAN.

1 Jun 1799, Fleming County: John FINLEY w Mary LONGHEAD.

28 Feb 1828, Madison County: John C. FINLEY w Arthusa HUFF.

22 Feb 1847, Fleming County: John P. FINLEY w Catharine CALLAHAN.

25 Mar 1830, Madison County: Martha FINLEY w Jonathan STREET.

15 Jan 1818, Hopkins County: Mary FINLEY w James BERRY.

7 Feb 1824, Christian County: Mary FINLEY w Isaac MEACHAM.

23 Sept 1805, Logan County: Mary FINLEY w Hugh ORR.

15 Oct 1821, Mason County: Mary FINLEY w Wallace SHANNON.

27 Dec 1868, Hopkins County: Mary E. FINLEY w James H. LAFFOON.

26 Nov 1857, Fulton County: Mary Jane FINLEY w Richard HARRIS.

5 Feb 1811, Mercer County: Nancy FINLEY w Josiah JONES.

26 Nov 1829, Mason County: Paulina FINLEY w Robert BUTLER.

26 Oct 1815, Christian County: Peggy T. FINLEY w Robert BRITT.

1 Jun 1814, Jessamine County: Polly FINLEY w Banoni P. DOWNING.

17 Feb 1816, Lincoln County: Polly FINLEY w Henry OWSLEY.

26 Apr 1792, Nelson County: Reuben FINLEY w Elizabeth KING.

20 Jan 1839, Lawrence County: Rhoda FINLEY w Henry STRATTEN.

28 May 1874, Casey County: Robert Z. FINLEY w Elizabeth MAY.

6 Jul 1805, Ohio County: Sam FINLEY w Sarah BIGGER.

10 Sept 1822, Fleming County: Samuel FINLEY w Mary PURDUM.

16 Jan 1804, Fayette County: Samuel FINLEY w Patsy WARDLOW.

15 Nov 1838, Pike County: Sophia FINLEY w James MAYNARD.

18 Dec 1813, Christian County: Thankful FINLEY w Joseph MEACHAM.

3 Jan 1828, Hopkins County: Thomas H. FINLEY w Maria MALIN.

23 Mar 1817, Lincoln County: William FINLEY w Sally BAIRD.

17 Sept 1817, Hopkins County: William FINLEY w Leah DOBYNS.

15 Aug 1851, Caldwell County: William FINLEY w D.A. MONEYMAKER.

27 Oct 1790, Mercer County: William FINLEY w Martha MC BRIDE.

GEORGIA MARRIAGES; Submitter: Florence NELSON

4 Feb 1838, Butts County: Thomas P. FENDLEY w Mary Ann MC LANE.

2 Jun 1835, Coveta County: Michael FENDLEY w Mary GRAY.

3 May 1804, Greene County: John FENDLEY w Mary RAY.

23 Jan 1840, Greene County: Leroy I. FENDLEY w Hannah WOODHAM.

1 Jan 1840, Greene County: Norwood H. FENDLEY w Cynthia CALDWELL.

26 Nov 1802, Greene County: Robert FENDLEY w Jane FINDLEY.

18 Aug 1802, Greene County: Robert FENDLEY w Lucinda FINDLEY.

5 Feb 1801, Greene County: Thomas FENDLEY w Margaret ALLEN.

9 Nov 1823, Greene County: Thomas FENDLEY w Ann WAGGONER.

3 Aug 1846, Greene County: Thomas FENDLEY w Nancy GREGORY.

17 Aug 1869, Greene County: Thomas L. FENDLEY w C.A. CRAWFORD.

29 Jun 1805, Greene County: William FENDLEY w Polly SHARP.

8 Dec 1812, Oglethorpe County: L.H. FINDLEY w Elizabeth SMITH.

13 Sept 1810, Oglethorpe County: Rainey FINDLEY w Nancy MARTIN.

17 Feb 1817, Oglethorpe County: Samuel FINDLEY w Sally MITCHELL.

29 May 1821, Oglethorpe County: James FINLEY w Mary WRAY.

22 Oct 1849, Oglethorpe County: Oliver FINLEY w Margaret CAMPBELL.

10 Mar 1831, Fayette County: James FENLEY w Martha YATES.

11 Apr 1847, Gilmer County: James J. FENDLEY w Elizabeth STEPHENS.

10 Jun 1830, Henry County: Ackeson FENDLY w Rebecca CLEMENTS.

6 Jul 1837, Henry County: Robert FENDLY w Tabitha HILL.

7 Apr 1839, Henry County: Samuel FENLEY w Ann DAVIS.

21 Mar 1833, Jackson County: Dempsey FENLEY w Judith S. VENABLE.

13 Dec 1836, Jasper County: John M. FENLEY w Eda HOLLAND.

4 Jul 1827, Jasper County: Alfred FINLEY w Ruth HOWARD.

10 Oct 1833, Jasper County: Riley FINLEY w Margaret Eliza CURRY.

5 Oct 1803, Jasper County: Richard FINDLEY w Matilda ELLENSON.

19 Sept 1811, Jasper County: Henry FINDLEY w Mary BARRETT.

Part 9: Some Clan Genealogies

According to Stout there was an ancient "Clan Fionnladh" (Fionnlaigh) predating Clan Farquharson from which we are descended. Some say the name Finley is derived from the Gaelic names Fionnlaoch or Finlocha meaning "Fair hero." It first appeared according to the Ancient Genealogies around 200 BC. Stout says it is derived from the Gaelic Finnladh which meand "son of Fergus".

Stout's source for the ancient genealogies was the manuscript "Pedigrees" at the Society of Genealogy, London. According to him the clan Finley was outlawed after Macbeth was killed and as a result took on the name Farquharson for several generations. Eugenius MCFINLAY, a fourth son of Macbeth born around 1200 in Aberdeenshire , also known as Shaw Farquhar(son), was chief Clan Finley. This was the first use Farquharson in the ancient genealogies. I couldn't find any other use of the name Farquharson before or after this until the 1400's when the descendants of Ferquhard Shaw took the name of Farquharson from Ferquhard. The current Clan Farquharson is descended from this line.

In "Scottish Clans and Regiments", Sir Thomas Inns states: "The old Clan Fionnladh reemerged in the early part of the thirteenth century as one of the original 16 Clans of the "Hail Kin Clan Chattan"

Vol I of FINLEY FINDINGS INTERNATIONAL states: Because of this [Finley being outlawed] the Clan FIONNLAGH took on the name of the Clan FARQUHARSON, so named because of the Farquhar SHAW of Rothiemurchus. WOOD and FRANCE state: "In 1236 in the Braes of Mar at the head of Aberdeenshire, Scotland, there was a certain chief named FEARCHAR, son of FARQUHAR, who was the fourth son of Shaw DUBH of Rothiemurchus, who was head of a powerful clan known in the Highlands as Clan FIONNLAGH, a sept of the great confederation, Clan CHATTAN, which held large possessions which were acquired by marriage with the heiress of Invercauld and from this FEARCHAR.

Clan Farquharson was part of the Clan Chattan confederation which included Clan Shaw, Clan Macintosh, Macpherson, Macbean, Davidson and Clan Farquharson. The genealogies get very complicated at this point.

Shaw "Mor", great-grandson of Angus, 6th Chief of MacKintosh and Eva of Clan Chattan was, by tradition, the leader of Clan Chattan. His son, James, was killed at Harlaw in 1411 but his heir, Alasdair "Ciar" succeded him.

The Clan Farquharson page at tartans.com says: Clan Farquharson, of Celtic origin, derives from Farquhar, fourth son of Alexander "Ciar" Mackintosh of Rothiemurchus, 5th Chief of Clan Shaw. A grant of arms made by Lord Lyon in 1697 stated that John Farquharson of Invercauld was lawfully descended of Shaw son of MacDuff, Thane of Fife whose successors had the name Shaw until Farquhar Shaw, son to Shaw of Rothiemerchus, Chief of the whole name came to be called Farquharson. Thus the Farquharsons branched from Clan Shaw. Farquhar settled in the Braes of Mar and was appointed baillie or chamberlain thereof. It was Donald Farquharson who married Isobel Stewart, heiress of Invercauld and their son Finlay Mór, 1st of the House of Farquharson of Invercauld, who gave to the Farquharson Chiefs their style MacFionnlaidh (siol Fhionnlaidh or descendents of Finlay).

At Clan MacKintosh it states: "Angus [the 20th chief of MacKintosh], married Anne, daughter of Farquharson of Invercauld, a lady who distinguished herself greatly inthe rebelion of 1745."

William McKinley, 25th president of the United States, ancestors were also MacIntosh of clan Farquharson.

History of the Shaw/Seath Clan states: Shaw Macduff, a younger son of Duncan, Thane of Fife (a descendant of Kenneth mac Alpin) assisted King Malcolm IV in putting down a rebellion in Moray and he was made keeper of Inverness castle. Shaw's grandson was granted land in Rothiemurchus (in Strathspey). His son married a daughter of the Macdonald Lord of Islay in 1291.

Patricia Myers wrote: Farquhar Shaw, the fourth son of Alexander III, Shaw of Rothiemurchus, was the ancestor of Clan FARQUHARSON. His son married the heiress of Invercauld and the Clan gained its lands on Deeside. Its most famous chief was Farquhar, Finla Mor who consolidated the Clan and who carried the Royal Standard at the Battle of Pinkie in 1547 fighting for Mary, Queen of Scots." Castles Braemar Castle, was owned by the Farquharson family in 1731 and Invercauld Castle still is owned and occupied by the Farquharson family.

Invercauld Castle Braemar Castle Scotland Near Braemar, Aberdeenshire - Royal Deeside. The Farquharson estate which included both castles covers about 200,000 acres of forest and moor in the Grampian Highlands. Breamar castle sits across the River Dee from INVERCAULD Castle. The Clan Chief today is Capt. A. Farquharson of Invercauld, the 16th Chief. He and his wife live in Invercauld Castle. His wife is former Frances Rodney who use to be editor of Harper's Bazaar magazine and fashion editor of Vogue magaizine.

Directions: Braemar Castle, located ½ mile north of Braemar on the A93, is open April 10 to October 31, Saturday through Thursday from 10 to 6. To reach Braemar from Edinburgh follow the A90 over the Forth Road Bridge to the M90 heading north to Perth. Just before Perth take junction 10 to junction 11; then take the A93 exit to Braemar (approximately 90 miles from Edinburgh) Balmoral Castle, the summer home of the Royal Family, is 8 mi. North on A93.

Braemar Info. at Travel Lady, Invercauld Estate at SportingEstates.com Castle of Invercauld at scottishcastles-info, at Scottish-Castle-Holidays. Braemar Map at MultiMap, Aberdeenshire Map at Univ. of Edinburgh Roots A possible genealogy may go something like this. This is pieced together from several other histories Shaw, Mackintosh and Farquharson and cannot be confirmed.

Shaw MacDuff, son of the third Earl of Fife . Duncan (4th Earl of Fife) MacDuff (d. 1154)

.. Shaw Mackintosh, the first Chief of the Clan, died in 1179

... Shaw (d. 1210)

.... William

..... Shaw (d. 1265)

...... Farquhar MacKintosh

.... Angus ("Mor" Mackintosh) 6th Chief of MacKintosh (d. 1345)

.... +Eva, (m. 1291) descended from Gillichattan Mor and her father

was Gilpatric, or Dougal Dall

.... Ian-

.... Gilchrist-

.... Shaw "Mor" Mackintosh (fought at Perth in 1396)

.... James (d. 1411)

.... Alexander Cier (Alister "Ciar")(Shaw) of Rothiemurchus,

5th chief of Clan Shaw ... owner of the Braes of Mar in Aberdeenshire.

.... Farquhar

.... Donald Farquharson

.... +Isobel Stewart, heiress of Invercauld

.... Farquhar, Finla Mor (b. abt. 1487; d. 1547) Consolidated the Clan
and was killed at the Battle of Pinkie in 1547.

.... William Farquharson

.... Janet Farquharson

.... Alexander McComie

.... John McIntosh (d. 12 JAN 1676 in Crandart)

The Farquharson History at fiss.com. says they took the name Farquharson
from Ferquhard Shaw and gives the following lineage:

.... Shaw MacDuff

.... Shaw Corshiacalich (d. 1405 Rothiemurchus)

(Led the Chattan men in the Great Clan Battle

on the North Inch of Perth in 1396)

+daughter of Clinie MacPherson

.... Ferquhard Shaw (settled in the Brae Mar)

+ daughter of Patrick Donnacha

.... Ferchar Chief of Clan

+ daughter of the Chisholm of Strathglas

.... ?

.... Finnula Mor, or Great Findlay, (b. abt. 1487; d. 1547) died in Battle of Pinkie

+ Beatrice Gordon

.... John

See also: Finley Findings International, Finley Ancient History, Clan Farquharson pages at tartans.com. fiss.com/chattan, ElectricScotland.com and at clan-farquharson.com, ScotClans, Finley Farquharson Discussions, The Clan Farquharson of Invercauld, Clan Shaw and Shaw History. .

Part 10: Ruardri King of Moray Father of King MacBeth

Ruardri King of Moray

The identity of Raudri King of Moray / Findláech mac Ruadrí / Macruaidhri Thane- Máel Coluim of Moray (or Máel Coluim mac Máil Brigti) was King or Mormaer of Moray has been the subject of historic argument for centuries. This research is to look at all documentation and historic sources that may help in correctly identifying the parentage and ancestry of Raudri and his lineage.

As per my research the lineage for Ruadri goes as follows:

Generation 1 - Ruadri King of Moray or Findláech mac Ruadrí or Macruaidhri Thane

Notes from "The Royal House of Moray" -

Sometime in the century after the reign of Kenneth, the branch of the Tribe of Loarn headed by Ruadri moved into the province of Moray. Moray is the land south of the Moray Firth, around the present-day town of Elgin. The leader of the Moraymen was called a mormaer, which is a Celtic title equivalent to the Anglo-Scandinavian earl, which we use today.

The descent of the MacKays through the mormaers of Moray begins as follows: Ruadri was the son of Aircellach, king of Dalriada; this Ruadri had a son Cathmail, who had a son Donald, who had a son Morgan, who had a son Donald, who had a son Ruadri.

This latter Ruadri had three sons: Findlaech, Maelbrigte, and Donald. It is Donald who is believed to be the male ancestor of what was to become the Clan MacKay. The only evidence concerning Donald which we have is an addition to the mediæval Book of Deer. In it, we find written the following: "Donald, Ruadri's son, and Malcolm, Culen's son, gave Biffie to God and to Drostan." 6 What this means is that Donald gave title to land over to the Abbey of Deer, along with the younger son of Culen, the King of Scots from 967 to 971. This incident is referred to in Burke's Guide to the Royal Family, where the author notes "Malcolm, co-benefactor with Donald MacRuadri of Moray of the Abbey of Deer ca [around] 1000.

RUAIDHRI . MORMAER of Moray

m—-. The name of Ruaidhri's wife is not known.

Ruadhri & his wife had two children:

1. FINDLAECH MacRory (-[1018/20]). Thane of Angus, Mormaer of Moray.

Orkneyinga Saga records that Sigurd Jarl of Orkney defeated "a Scottish earl called Finnleik". The Annals of Tigernach record that "Findlaech mac Ruaidhrí mormaer Moreb" was killed "a filiis fratris sui MaelBrighdi" in [1018/20]. The Annals of Ulster record the death in 1020 of "Finnlaech son of Ruadrí king of Alba...killed by his own people"[480]. m—-. The name of Findlaech's wife is not known. Many secondary sources name the wife of Findlaech as Donada of Scotland, daughter of Malcolm II King of Scotland & his wife—-, adding that she was the mother of King Macbeth. It seems that the proof for this connection is slim. The only source so far identified which refers to Macbeth's maternal origin is the Chronicle of Huntingdon which names "Maket Regem [=King Macbeth] nepotem dicti Malcolmi" when recording that he was expelled from Scotland after ruling 15 years. The word "nepos" is of course treacherous and could indicate a variety of relationships in addition to grandson. However, it appears that early historians assumed that "grandson" was the correct translation. For example, Ralph Holinshed's 1577 Chronicle of Scotland names "Doada" as second daughter of Malcolm II King of Scotland and adds that she married "Sinell the thane of Glammis, by whom she had issue one Makbeth"[482]. Another variation is provided by the Cronykil of Andrew of Wyntoun, which records that "Makbeth-Fynlak, his systyr sowne" murdered King Duncan. From a chronological point of view, it is unlikely that Macbeth could have been a nephew of King Duncan, but it is possible that the passage represents an interpretation of "nepos" from an earlier source and has confused the king with whom Macbeth enjoyed this relationship. No source earlier than Holinshed has been found which names her Donada. Mormaer Findlaech & had one child:

a) MACBETH ([1005]-killed in battle Lumphanan, Aberdeenshire 15 Aug 1057, bur Isle of Iona). The 12th century Cronica Regum Scottorum lists "...Macheth filius Findleg xvii..." as king. The Annals of Tigernach names "Mac bethadh son of Findlaech overking of Scotland" when recording his death. Mormaer of Moray [1029/32]. He succeeded in 1040 as MACBETH King of Scotland. He was defeated in battle 27 Jul 1054 by the army of Siward Earl of Northumbria who had invaded Scotland to support the claim to the throne of Malcolm son of King Duncan I. The Annals of Ulster record that "Mac Bethad son of Finnlaech, over-king of Scotland was killed by Mael Sechlainn son of Donnchad in battle" in 1058. m ([after 1032]) [as her second husband,] GRUOCH, [widow of GILLACOMGAIN Mormaer of Moray,] daughter of BOITE [Bodhe] of Scotland & his wife -—([1015]-). "Machbet filius Finlach...et Gruoch filia Bodhe, rex et regina Scottorum" made grants to the church of St Serf, although the document also names "Malcolmus Rex filius Duncani" which casts doubt on its authenticity. Her possible first marriage appears to be based on the following logic. The Continuation of the Synchronisms of Flann Mainistreach records Lulach as son of Macbeth. The Annals of Ulster record that "Lulach son of Gilla Comgain, over-king of Scotland was killed in battle by Mael Coluim son of Donnchad" in 1058. Dunbar, basing his argument on this and the other sources which are quoted in this section, states that "from the above it seems most probable that Lulach was son of Gillacomgan and step-son of Macbeth". In addition, the 12th century Cronica Regum Scottorum lists "Lulac nepos filii Boide" ["nephew of the son of Boite"] as successor of King Macbeth. However, there does not appear to be a surviving source which more specifically confirms that Macbeth´s queen was the widow of Gillacomgain and mother of Lulach.

http://en.wikipedia.org/wiki/Clan_Gregor

2. MAELBRIGTE . The Annals of Tigernach record that "Findlaech mac Ruaidhrí mormaer Moreb" was killed "a filiis fratris sui MaelBrighdi" in [1018/ 20]. m—-. The name of Maelbrigte´s wife is not known. Maelbrigte & his wife had two children:

http://hal_macgregor.tripod.com/gregor/pictclanns.htm

[According to tradition]: MacBethad, son of Findláech, son of Ruadrí, son of Domnall, son of Morggán, son of Cathamal, son of Ruadrí, son of Ailgelach, son of Uraad, son of Uurgus, son of Nehhtonn, son of Colmán, son of Báetán, son of Eochaid, son of Muiredach, son of Loarn, son of Erb, son of Eochaid Muinremuir. MacBeth (1005-1057), Mormaer of Moray, married Gruoch, daughter of Boedhe, who was the son of Kenneth III. So MacBeth, who had ancestral roots in Moray, was the grandson of King Malcolm II, and his wife was the granddaughter of King Kenneth III.

Under the ancient law of the Picts, he had as much claim to the throne of Scotland as did King Duncan I. He was commander for Duncan I, whom he defeated and slew, thereby becoming king. MacBeth was proclaimed king, and Scotland prospered during his reign. He was later defeated by Malcolm, the son of Duncan. Malcolm had gone to England to raise funds and an army to bring about MacBeth's downfall. His debt to the English would have disastrous effects on Scotland for years to come.

It is a generally held opinion by Scottish historians that if MacBeth had not been killed by the future King Malcolm III, Scotland would probably have remained a separate nation until this day and might have conquered England. Records show that he used his power for the good of his country. His reign verifies that Picts actually ruled Albann after Kenneth MacAlpin.

In Angus, 'MacBeths' received a charter from David II in 1369, but this family was of the ancestral line of the Fife Bethunes, who anciently held lands in the area. The later history of the MacBeths, the Highland Beatons and Bethunes has become hopelessly confused for, in the various lands with which they are associated, both forms were used, often referring to the same family, sometimes even to the same person. Others duly removed to the shires of Inverness, Sutherland & Easter Ross and the name was also found in Moray where they had association with the Macbeans.

The name of this clan will always have overtones of Shakespeare's tragic Scottish king. The real MacBeth ruled 1040 to 1057,and had little in common with the villainous figure portrayed in he play. He had a valid claim to the throne and slew his rival on he battlefield, not in the bed chamber. He ruled wisely and generously, finding time to make a pilgrimage to Rome, where he scattered money among the poor like seed. He did in fact die in battle, at Lumphanan - not when Birnam Wood moved to Dunsinane as Shakespeare wrote.

The MacBeths of Moray were the principle branch of the clan, while the Bethunes and Beatons were secondary. The king was christened with 'MacBeth' (anglicized) as his Christian name, as surnames were not mandatory at that time. Mac Beatha means son of life in Gaelic, so the official Scottish version at the time would have been MacBeathad mac Findláich. MacBeth was the last Celtic Ruler of Albann/Scotland. After him, a series of anti-Celtic programs were initiated to forcibly transplant Northern Picts to Welsh speaking areas of Scotland.

Upon MacBeth's death, the name of his beloved Albann was changed to 'Scotland' as the title of Monarch was changed from the P-Celtic 'Ri Albainn' to the Latin 'Rex Scotorum'.

Generation 2 - Cuiléain mac Iduilb or Indulf Another name for Indulf is Idulb mac Causantín

(Scottish : Idulb mac Causantín) was king of Scotland from 954 until 962, although there is no record of his coronation, if there ever was one. He was son of King Constantine II, second cousin of the previous king Malcolm I, and second cousin first removed of his successor Dubh.

The name Idulb is a Gaelicisation of either the Old Norse name Hildulfr or the Anglo-Saxon name Eadulf. Idulb later became rendered Indulf under French influence.

During his reign, a rebirth of Danish invasions began. These visits, which were growing more familiar but not more welcome, came to brace the patriotism of the nation when in danger of becoming relaxed. The Norsemen crossed the sea in a fleet of fifty ships. They ravaged the southern shores of England. Intent, however on gathering more booty before returning to their own country, they sailed northward and entered the Firth of Forth. Their appearance spread terror along both shores of the Firth. The timid left their houses and fled. The courageous hastened to the beach and mustered in such force that the Danes deemed it prudent to withdraw. Dropping down the Firth past the Isle of May, their galleys crept round the "neuk" of Fife and entered the Firth of Tay. Again, a phalanx of determined combatants lined the shores of the river and the invaders saw that there was no safe landing place. They sailed away, and coasting along the shores of Angus and Mearns, they arrived off Buchan, searching all the way for an unguarded creek or bay into which they might run their galleys and let loose their ravaging hordes like a flock of vultures upon the land. The coast bristled with defenders ready to grapple with the foe should he dare to land and throw him back into the waves. The invaders put their helms about and bore away to the Danish shore. It was a feint. After vanishing in the blue, they suddenly reappeared. Finding the coast unguarded, they landed unopposed in Banffshire near Cullen. Brief time was given them to pillage and slay. Indulf soon came up with them and the two armies were installed in combat. The Danes were worsted and driven to their ships and hoisting sail, this time in earnest, they made off to their own country.

Indulf left one lasting contribution. His father, Constantine II, fleeing before Athelstan, had abandoned the Lothian, and with the Lothians a city destined one day to be the capital of Scotland, to the English. In a decisive victory over Edwin of Deira, Indulf recaptured the fortress in Edinburgh, Dun Eden.

Indulf married at some point in his life, but the details are scanty. The date and place of the marriage are unrecorded, and the name of his wife is similarly unknown. He had three sons, all of whom later died violently in separate engagements.

Like his father before him, Indulf at least intended to abdicate and become a monk. Conflicting accounts state that he was killed by invading Vikings in 962 at the Battle of the Bauds in Findochty, Banffshire. It is unclear whether at the time he was still king or if he had already abdicated.

His son, Culen, later became king in 966.

Generation 3 - Causantín mac Áeda

Constantine II (Causantín mac Áeda) (874 ?- 952) was king of Scotland from 900 to 943. He was the son of King Aedh, first cousin of the previous King

Donald II, and first cousin once removed of his successor Malcolm I, to whom he left his kingdom upon abdicating and becoming a monk. Constantine II's reign is the second longest reign in Scottish history.

Constantine II succeeded Donald II to the Scottish throne in 900. If a coronation took place, then there is no surviving record of it.

During his reign, Constantine II had to fend off Viking raids from the north and west. The earliest of these involved driving the Vikings away from Scotland, and this reached a triumphant climax at the Battle of Scone in 904, after which the Vikings were forced to withdraw from Scotland. However, by then, the Vikings had laid waste to much of Scotland, and in particular Dunkeld.

Constantine II later struggled to win land from, or at least not lose land to, his neighbours to the south, the Anglo-Saxons earldom of Northumbria and the Norse kingdom of York, where the Vikings, led by the Viking king Rognvald, had resettled themselves. Constantine II and the Earl of Bamburgh, Ealdred I, were involved in two battles with Rognvald Gudrodsson (referred to as the Battles of Corbridge) in that area in 915 and 918, both of which resulted ultimately in a cessation of hostilities there with the Norse.

When he was not involved in fighting Vikings, Constantine II remodelled the Christian church of the day to be more Gaelic in nature. This included a Synod at Scone in 906 , and he introduced the mormaer (earls) system to Scotland. Constantine II married at some point in his life, but virtually nothing is known of it. The date and place of the marriage are unrecorded, and his wife's name is likewise forgotten. It is known, however, that the marriage produced at least three children: two sons and a daughter.

Constantine II's daughter, whose name is also no longer known, married Olaf III Guthfrithson, the Norse King of Dublin at the time, in 937, in order to establish a more stable relationship with the Norse. At least three children later came from this marriage. If it was intended to contribute to holding back Northumbria, it did not. Constantine II was defeated at the Battle of Brunanburh by King Athelstan of England in 937. One of Constantine II's sons, Cellach, died in this battle.

In 943, Constantine II abdicated in favour of Malcolm I (943-954) and entered a Culdee monastery in St Andrews, Fife, and eventually became Abbot there. He died peacefully in 952, and was probably buried at the monastery. Constantine II's surviving son, Indulf, later became King of Scotland.

Generation 4 - Áeda mac Causantín Other names for Aed were Aedh and Aodh.

Aed (c. 840 - 878), sometimes spelt Aedh or Aodh, became King of Scots in 877 when he succeeded his brother Constantine I of Scotland.

He was killed shortly after taking the throne by Giric of Scotland, also known as Gregory the Great, who had conspired with Aedh's nephew, Eochaid of Scotland.

Not much is known of Aedh, or even if he was actually the one named by Constantine to hold the throne. Both Giric and Eochaid ruled jointly following Aedh's death.

Aedh did marry at some point in his life, but the details, including the date and place of the marriage, and the name of his wife are not known. One son, Constantine II of Scotland, ruled later (900-942/43), while another son, Donald mac Aed, became King of Strathclyde in 908.

Aedh died violently in 878 at Strathallan, Perth and Kinross. He may have been buried at Maiden Stone in Aberdeenshire. He was succeeded under the Scottish tanistry system by his nephew, Eochaid.

Generation 5 - Causantín mac Domnall or Máel Coluim Mac Domnaill

Máel Coluim mac Domnaill (Modern Gaelic : Maol Chaluim mac Dhòmhnaill),[1] anglicised as Malcolm I, and nicknamed An Bodhbhdercc, "the Dangerous Red"[2] (before 900 - 954) was king of Scots , becoming king when his cousin Constantine II (Causantín mac Áeda) abdicated to become a monk. He was the son of Donald II (Domnall mac Causantín).

In 945 Edmund the Elder , King of England, having expelled Olaf Sihtricsson (Amlaíb Cuaran) from Northumbria , devastated Cumbria and blinded two sons of Domnall III (Domnall mac Eógain), king of Strathclyde . It is said that he then "let" or "commended" Strathclyde to Malcolm in return for an alliance.[3] What is to be understood by "let" or "commended" is unclear, but it may well mean that Malcolm had been the overlord of Strathclyde and that Edmund recognised this while taking lands in southern Cumbria for himself.

The Chronicle of the Kings of Alba says that Malcolm took an army into Moray "and slew Cellach". Cellach is not named in the surviving genealogies of the rulers of Moray , and his identity is unknown.

Malcolm appears to have kept his agreement with the late English king, which may have been renewed with the new king, Edmund having been murdered in 946 and succeeded by his brother Edred . Eric Bloodaxe took York in 948, before being driven out by Edred, and when Olaf Sihtricsson again took York in 949-950, Malcolm raided Northumbria as far south as the Tees taking "a multitude of people and many herds of cattle" according to the Chronicle.[6] The Annals of Ulster for 952 report a battle between "the men of Alba and the Britons [of Strathclyde] and the English" against the foreigners, i.e. the Northmen or the Norse-Gaels . This battle is not reported by the Anglo-Saxon Chronicle, and it is unclear whether it should be related to the expulsion of Olaf Sihtricsson from York or the return of Eric Bloodaxe.

The Annals of Ulster report that Malcolm was killed in 954. Other sources place this most probably in the Mearns , either at Fetteresso following the Chronicle, or at Dunnottar following the Prophecy of Berchán . He was buried on Iona .[8] Malcolm's sons Dub and Kenneth were later kings.

Noted events in his life were:

• Crowned: King of Scots, 943.

His children were:

+ 2 M i. Cinaed King of Scots 3 4 5 was born about 932 in Scotland, died in 995 in <Fettercairn, (Aberdeenshire), Scotland> about age 63, and was buried in Iona, Argyllshire, Scotland.

+ 3 M ii. Dub of Scotland 6 died about 967.

DONALD (-killed Dun-fother [900], bur [Isle of Iona]). The 10th century Pictish Chronicle Cronica de Origine Antiquorum Pictorum records that "Donivaldus filius Constantini" reigned for eleven years, after the expulsion of Eochlaid[46]. The 11th century Synchronisms of Flann Mainistreach name (in order) "Cinaet mac Ailpin...Domnall mac Ailpin, Custantin mac Cinaeta, (Aedh mac Cinaedha), Girg mac Dungaile, Domnall Dasachtach (mac Custantin)" as Scottish kings, dated to the 9th and 10th centuries. The 12th century Cronica Regum Scottorum lists "...Duneval filius Constantini xi..." as king. The Chronicle of John of Fordun records that "Donald...the son of...Constantine, son of Kenneth the Great" succeeded in 892 after the death of Gregory and reigned for eleven years. He succeeded his cousin as DONALD II "Dasachtach" King of Scotland. The 10th century Pictish Chronicle Cronica de Origine Antiquorum Pictorum records that the Scots defeated the Danes during Donald's reign, and that he was killed "opidum Fother". The Annals of Ulster record the death in 900 of "Domnall son of Constantine king of Scotland". The Chronicle of the Scots and Picts dated 1177 records that "Donald mac Constantine" reigned for 11 years, died "in Fores" and was buried "in Iona insula". The Chronicle of the Picts and Scots dated 1251 includes the same information.

Additional notes:

Named for sept of the Clann Cheallaigh (e.g. Mac Domhnaill or Mac Donnell). Ceann Coradh, now Kincora, was the stronghold of Brian, near the mouth of the Shannon river. For 1031, Diarmait, mac Domhnaill, mic Faoláin, king of the Deisi. The names of the Gallowglass who then came and remained in the county are: in Connacht – Mac Domhnaill, Mac Ruaidhri and Mac Suibhne.

O'Cannon, ousted as kings of Cenél Conaill in the 13th century, settled here for a time here. Arda Midhair, The Ó Dochartaigh (O'Dohertys), of Cenél Conaill, were cited as chiefs of Arda Midhair (Ardmire, perhaps the Finn Valley) in the barony of Raphoe, county Donegal. At the turn of the 13th century two Ó Dochartaigh were noted as kings of Tír Chonaill, breaking a long hold the O'Cannons and O'Muldorys (Mulderrys) had on this title.

Early prominent septs of Cenél Aedha in the area of Tirhugh included Ó Maeldoraidh, Ó Canannáin (O'Cannon) and Ó Gallchobhair (O'Gallagher).

MacDonnell of Clan Celleagh

Generation 6 - Domnall mac Causantín

Domnall macCausantín (anglicised Donald II) was King of the Picts or King of Alba in the late 9th century. He was the son of Causantín mac Cináeda. Domnall is given the epithet dásachtach by the Prophecy of Berchán, meaning a violent madman. Domnall became king on the death or depositionof Giric mac Dúngail, the date of which is not certainly known but usually placed in 889. The Chronicle of the Kings of Alba reports:

Doniualdus son of Constantini held the kingdom for 11 years [889 - 900]. The Northmen wasted Pictland at this time. In his reign a battle occurred between Danes and Scots at Innisibsolian where the Scots had victory. He was killed at Opidum Fother [modern Dunnottar] by the Gentiles. It has been suggested that the attack on Dunottar, rather than being a small raid by a handful of pirates, may be associated with the ravaging of Scotland attributed to Harald Fairhair in the Heimskringla.[3] The Prophecy of Berchán places Domnall's death at Dunnottar, but appears to attribute it to Gaels rather than Norsemen; other sources report he died at Forres. Domnall's death is dated to 900 by the Annals of Ulster and the Chronicon Scotorum, where he is called king of Alba, rather that king of the Picts. He was buried on Iona.

The change from king of the Picts to king of Alba is seen as indicating a step towards the kingdom of the Scots, but historians, while divided as to when this change should be placed, do not generally attribute it to Domnall in view of his epithet. The consensus view is that the key changes occurred in the reign of Causantín mac Áeda, but the reign of Giric has also been proposed. The Chronicle of the Kings of Alba has Domnall succeeded by his cousin Causantín mac Áeda. Domnall's son Máel Coluim was later king. The Prophecy of Berchán appears to suggest that another king reigned for a short while between Domnall and Causantín, saying "half a day will he take sovereignty". Possible confirmation of this exists in the Chronicon Scotorum, where the death of "Ead, king of the Picts" in battle against the Uí Ímair is reported in 904. This, however, is thought to be an error, referring perhaps to Ædwulf, the ruler of Bernicia, whose death is reported in 913 by the other Irish annals.

Generation 7 - Caustantín mac Cinaeda son of Fergus

Caustantín or Constantín mac Fergusa (English: Constantine son of Fergus) (before 775–820) was king of the Picts (or of Fortriu), in modern Scotland, from 789 until 820. He was until the Victorian era sometimes counted as Constantine I of Scotland; the title is now generally given to Constantín mac Cináeda. He is credited with having founded the church at Dunkeld which later received relics of St Columba from Iona.

It had been proposed that Constantín and his brother Óengus were sons of Fergus mac Echdach, King of Dál Riata, but this is no longer widely accepted. Instead, it is thought they were kin to the first king Óengus mac Fergusa, perhaps grandsons or grandnephews. This family may have originated in Circinn (presumed to correspond with the modern Mearns) and had with ties to the Eóganachta of Munster in Ireland.

Constantín's reign falls in a period when Irish annals have relatively few notices of events in Scotland, possibly due to the failing of the annals believed to have been kept in Scotland at Iona and Applecross. Perhaps for that reason, there are only two reports which mention him. Other entries make it clear that the Vikings were active in Ireland and on the western coasts of Scotland in this time, which may also account for the lack of records. Iona was a target, and it may be that Abbot Noah of Kingarth, on the Isle of Bute, was killed by raiders.

The first report, in 789, is the record of a battle in Pictland between Constantín and Conall mac Taidg, in which Constantín was victorious. Conall later reappears in Kintyre, where was killed in 807. It is not known whether Constantín was king before defeating Conall. The king lists give varying lengths for his reign, from 35 to 45 years, and are not to be relied upon without independent confirmation.[6] The second report is that of Constantín's death in 820..

The Dupplin Cross was long assumed to commemorate Cináed mac Ailpín's final victory over the Picts, as indeed, was Sueno's Stone. Recent analysis has revealed a small part of an inscription on the Cross, in which Constantín is named. Accordingly, it is supposed that this monument was commissioned by him, or as a memorial to him. He appears there as Custantin filius Fircus[sa], a Latinisation derived from the Old Irish version of his name rather than the presumed Pictish form Castantin filius Uurguist found in the Poppleton Manuscript and similar Pictish king lists. The Martyrology of Tallaght (University College Dublin Ms. A3) from the Book of Leinster, c. 1180.

It has been proposed that the St Andrews Sarcophagus was made for Constantín, but this is a minority view, as is the suggestion that the relics of Columba, perhaps including the Monymusk Reliquary, may have been translated from Iona to Dunkeld uring Constantín's reign.[8] The idea that Columba's relics may have come to Dunkeld in the time of Constantín, rather than thirty years later in the time of Cináed mac Ailpín is based on an entry in the Chronicon Scotorum for 818

That Constantín established Dunkeld is stated by later chroniclers such as John of Fordun who are following some variants of the Pictish king lists or other materials now lost. Andrew of Wyntoun dates the foundation to 815, although he states that this was after the deaths of Charlemagne and Pope Leo III, which would date it to 816 or later. It is suggested that Constantín is commemorated by the Martyrology of Tallaght, a product of one of the principal céli dé monasteries of the day. As a patron of the céli dé, and perhaps a collaborator of Abbot Diarmait of Iona, it is thought that Constantín may have been a church reformer, in line with céli dé ideals.Caustantín appears also to have been a patron of the Northumbrian monasteries, as he is commemorated, along with his nephew Eogán, in the Liber Vitae Dunelmensis, which contains a list of those for whom prayers were said, dating from around 840.

Constantín was succeeded by his brother Óengus. His son Drest was later king. Constantín's son Domnall is believed to have been king of Dál Riata from around 811 until 835. Constantín's reputation among the kings who followed him may, perhaps, be demonstrated using his name on for three kings in the century and a half following his death when it is not attested as a kingly name in Scotland prior to his reign.

Generation 8 - Fergus mac Echdach

Fergus mac Echdach was king of Dál Riata (modern western Scotland) from about 778 until 781.

Scotland at the beginning of recorded history was composed of the kingdom of Picts in the north, awith other warlike tribes in their vincinity; the kingdom of the Scots, or Dalriada from Ireland in the west, later called Argyll; the Cymric, or Welsh, in the southwest called the kingdom of the Strathclyde Britons; and the Angles in the southeast. The English domain included the part of Scotland called Lothian and the northern part of England which for many years was contested betweenthe two countries. Gaelic was spoken by both the Picts and the Scots. Each of these regions were in constant warfare with the others, but with the union of the Picts and Dalriada Scots came a kingdom whichabsorbed the Welsh and Englaish region south of it.

(ref: http://en.wikipedia.org/wiki/Alpin_II_of_Dalriada) Alpín mac Echdach may refer to two persons, or to one, or to none. The first person is a presumed king of Dál Riata in the late 730s. The second is the father of Cináed mac Ailpín. The name Alpín is taken to be a Pictish one, derived from the Anglo-Saxon name Æelfwine; Alpín's patronymic means son of Eochaid or son of Eochu. Irish annals such as the Annals of Ulster and the Annals of Innisfallen name Cináed's father as one Alpín. This much is reasonably certain.

The Chronicle of the Kings of Alba usually begins with Cináed, but some variants include a reference to Cináed's father: "[Alpín] was killed in Galloway, after he had entirely destroyed and devastated it. Andthen the kingdom of the Scots was transferred to the kingdom [variant: land] of the Picts." John of Fordun (IV, ii) calls Cináed's father"Alpin son of Achay" (Alpín son of Eochu) and has him killed in war with the Picts; Andrew of Wyntoun's version mixes Fordun's war with thePicts with the Chronicle version which has him killed in Galloway.

The genealogies produced for Kings of Scots in the High Middle Ages traced their ancestry through Cináed mac Ailpín, through the Cenél nGabráin of Dál Riata to Fergus Mór, and then to legendary Irish kings such as Conaire Mor. These genealogies, perhaps oral in origin, were subjected to some regularisation by the scribes who copied them into sources such as the Chronicle of Melrose, the Poppleton Manuscript, and the like. Either by accident, or by design, several kings were misplaced, being moved from the early 8th century to the late 8th and early 9th century. The original list is presumed to have resembled the following:

1. Eochaid mac Domangairt

2. Ainbcellach mac Ferchair

3. Eógan mac Ferchair

4. Selbach mac Ferchair

5. Eochaid mac Echdach

6. Dúngal mac Selbaig

7. Alpín

8. Muiredach mac Ainbcellaig

9. Eógan mac Muiredaig

10. Áed Find

11. Fergus mac Echdach

After modification to link this list of kings of Dál Riata to the family of Cináed mac Ailpín, the list is presumed to have been in this form:

1. Eochaid mac Domangairt

2. Ainbcellach mac Ferchair

3. Eógan mac Ferchair

8. Muiredach mac Ainbcellaig

9. Eogan mac Muiredaig

10. Áed Find

11. Fergus mac Echdach

4. Selbach mac Ferchair (called Selbach mac Eógain)

5. Eochaid mac Echdach (called Eochaid mac Áeda Find)

6. Dúngal mac Selbaig (name unchanged)

7. Alpín (called Alpín mac Echdach)

However, the existence of the original Alpín is less than certain. Noking in Dál Riata of that name is recorded in the Irish annals in theearly 730s. A Pictish king named Alpín, whose father's name is not given in any Irish sources, or even from the Pictish Chronicle king-lists, is known from the late 720s, when he was defeated by Óengus mac Fergusa and Nechtan mac Der-Ilei. For the year 742, the Annals of Ulster are read was referring to the capture of "Elffin son of Crop" (the former reading had besieged rather than captured). Whether Álpin son of Crup is related to the Álpin of the 720s is unknown.

He succeeded Áed Find. He is stated to have been a son of Eochaid mac Echdach, and thus a brother of Áed. Some much later sources make him a son of Áed, but this is not credited by modern studies. His death is noticed in 781 by the Annals of Ulster.

Generation 9 - Eochaid mac Echdach

Eochaid mac Eochaid was king of Dál Riata (modern western Scotland) from 726 until 733. He was a son of Eochaid mac Domangairt.

Eochaid came to power as king of Dál Riata in 726, presumably deposing Dúngal mac Selbaig. Selbach may have tried to restore his son to power, and fought against Eochaid's supporters at Irros Foichnae in 727, but without apparent success. The annals vary as to whether the despatch of a fleet from Dál

Riata to Ireland to aid Flaithbertach mac Loingsig in his war with Áed Allán should be placed in the reign of Eochaid, or that of his successor.

At his death in 733, Eochaid is named king rather than lord of Dál Riata, which may suggest that after the defeat of Dúngal and Selbach his reign was unchallenged. His son, Áed Find, was later king of Dál Riata.

As Dál Riata certainly maintained a separate existence until 736, Eochaid must have had a successor, or successors. It appears that he was succeeded by Muiredach mac Ainbcellaig, who had replaced Dúngal mac Selbaig as king of the Cenél Loairn.

Generation 10 - Eochaid mac Domangart

Eochaid mac Domangairt (died ca. 697) was a king of Dál Riata (modern western Scotland) in about 697. He was a member of the Cenél nGabráin, the son of Domangart mac Domnaill and father of Eochaid mac Echdach; Alpín mac Echdach may also be a son of this Eochaid.

He is named in Dál Riata king-lists, the Duan Albanach and the Synchronisms of Flann Mainistrech. In some sources he is called Eochaid Crook-Nose (Riannamail), but modern readings take this is a being a garbled reference to Fiannamail ua Dúnchado rather than an epithet.

The killing of Eochu nepos Domnaill, Eochaid grandson of Domnall Brecc, is reported in the Annals of Ulster for 697.

Generation 11 - Domangart mac Domnall

Domangart mac Domnaill (died 673) was a king in Dál Riata (modern western Scotland) and the son of Domnall Brecc. It is not clear whether he was over-king of Dál Riata or king of the Cenél nGabráin.

Domangart is not listed by the Duan Albanach but is included in other sources, such as genealogies of William the Lion, and that of Causantín mac Cuilén found with the Senchus fer n-Alban. In these genealogies he is noted as the father of Eochaid mac Domangairt.

The Annals of Ulster for 673 report: "The killing of Domangart, son of Domnall Brecc, the king of Dál Riata." Some king-lists state that in his time the Cenél Comgaill separated from the Cenél nGabráin.

It is not clear who succeeded Domangart as king of Dál Riata, if he was such, or as king of the Cenél nGabráin. Known kings after Domangart include Máel Dúin mac Conaill and Domnall Donn of the Cenél nGabráin and Ferchar Fota of the Cenél Loairn is assigned a long reign of 21 years by the Duan Albanach and other king-lists, and this would place the beginning of his rule close to the death of Domangart.

Generation 12 - Domnall mac Echdach or Domnall Brecc

Domnall Brecc (Welsh: Dyfnwal Frych; English: Donald the Freckled) (d. 642 in Strathcarron) was king of Dál Riata, in modern Scotland, from about 629 until 642. He was the son of Eochaid Buide.

He first appears in 622, when the Annals of Tigernach report his presence at the battle of Cend Delgthen (probably in the east midlands of Ireland) as an ally of Conall Guthbinn of Clann Cholmáin. This is the only battle known where Domnall Brecc fought on the winning side.

Domnall suffered four defeats after he broke Dál Riata's alliance with the Cenél Conaill clan of the Uí Néill. In Ireland, Domnall and his ally Congal Cáech of the Dál nAraidi were defeated by Domnall mac Áedo of the Cenél Conaill, the High King of Ireland, at the Battle of Mag Rath (Moira, County Down) in 637. He also lost to the Picts in 635 and 638 and lastly to Eugein I of Alt Clut at Strathcarron in 642, where he was killed.

A stanza interpolated into the early 9th Century Welsh poem Y Gododdin refers to these events:

I saw an array that came from Pentir,

And bore themselves splendidly around the conflagration.

I saw a second one, rapidly descending from their township,

Who had risen at the word of the grandson of Nwython.[1]

I saw great sturdy men who came with the dawn,

And the head of Dyfnwal Frych, ravens gnawed it.

Domnall's son Domangart mac Domnaill was later to be king of Dál Riata and from him the later kings of the Cenél nGabráin were descended. A second son, Cathasach, died c. 650, and a grandson of Domnall, also called Cathasach, died c. 688.

Generation 13 - Eochaid mac Áedán or Eochaid Buide

Eochaid Buide was king of Dál Riata from around 608 until 629. "Buide" refers to the colour yellow, as in the colour of his hair.

He was a younger son of Áedán mac Gabráin and became his father's chosen heir upon the death of his elder brothers. Adomnán's Life of Saint Columba has Columba foresee that Eochaid, then a child, will succeed his father in preference to his adult brothers Artúr, Eochaid Find and Domangart.

In the last two years of his reign, 627–629, Eochaid was apparently co-ruler with Connad Cerr, who predeceased him. Eochaid was followed by his son Domnall Brecc.

Eochaid's other sons named by the Senchus fer n-Alban are Conall Crandomna, Failbe (who died at the Battle of Fid Eoin), Cú-cen-máthair (whose death is reported in the Annals of Ulster for 604), Conall Bec, Connad or Conall Cerr (who may be the same person as Connad Cerr who died at Fid Eoin), Failbe, Domangart and Domnall Donn (not the same person as Domnall Donn unless his obituary is misplaced by 45 years like that of Ferchar mac Connaid)

According to the Fled Dúin na nGéd, Eochaid Buide was the grandfather of Congal Cáech. The story has anachronistic features as it has Eochaid alive at the time of the battle of Mag Rath (securely dated to within a year of 637), but it is chronologically feasible that Congal Cáech could have been the son of

Eochaid's daughter if the identification of Cú-cen-máthair and the dating of his death is correct.

Generation 14 - Áedán mac Gabráin

Áedán mac Gabráin (pronounced [ˈaiðaːn mak ˈɡavraːnʲ] in Old Irish) was a king of Dál Riata from circa 574 until his death, perhaps on 17 April 609. The kingdom of Dál Riata was situated in modern Argyll and Bute, Scotland, and parts of County Antrim, Ireland. Genealogies record that Áedán was a son of Gabrán mac Domangairt.

He was a contemporary of Saint Columba, and much that is recorded of his life and career comes from hagiography such as Adomnán of Iona's Life of Saint Columba. Áedán appears as a character in Old Irish and Middle Irish language works of prose and verse, some now lost.

The Irish annals record Áedán's campaigns against his neighbours, in Ireland, and in northern Britain, including expeditions to the Orkney Islands, the Isle of Man, and the east coast of Scotland. As recorded by Bede, Áedán was decisively defeated by Æthelfrith of Bernicia at the Battle of Degsastan. Áedán may have been deposed, or have abdicated, following this defeat.

Generation 15 - Gabrán mac Domangairt

Gabrán mac Domangairt was king of Dál Riata in the middle of the 6th century. He is the eponymous ancestor of the Cenél nGabráin.

The historical evidence for Gabrán is limited to the notice of his death in the Irish annals. It is possible that his death should be linked to a migration or flight from Bridei mac Maelchon, but this may be no more than coincidence.

The king lists show Gabrán as the successor of his brother Comgall (d. ca. 537), and as the predecessor of Comgall's son Conall. The Duan Albanach gives him only a two year reign [Duan Albanach, 131], while the Latin Lists give 22 years [Poppleton MS, KKES, 253; Lists "D", "F", pp. 264, 270; probably correct] or 34 years [List "I", ibid., 281, probably an error for the 34 assigned to his son Áedán; Gabrán is accidently omitted by List "K", ibid., 286].

Date of Birth: Unknown. Place of Birth: Unknown.

Date of Death: d. ca. 559. ["... & mors Gabrain mc. Domangairt." AU (s.a. 559, also a duplicate entry s.a. 557); "Bass Gabrain maic Domanguirt ríg Alban." AT 17: 142; "Mors Gabráin mic Domangoirt, Rí Alban." CS, 52] Place of Death: Unknown.

Father: Domangart mac Fergusa, d. ca. 506?, king of Dál Riata.

Mother: Uncertain. See the Commentary section.

Spouse: Unknown. See the Commentary section.

Children: His five sons are named by Senchus Fer nAlban ["Cúic meic immora la Gabrán .i. Áedán. Éoganán. Cuildach Domnall. Domangart." Senchus, 41]. Only two of these sons are known from other sources.

MALE Áedán mac Gabráin, d. ca. 604, king of Dál Riata, ca. 573-ca. 604.

MALE Eóganán mac Gabráin, d. ca. 593. ["Mors Eugain m. Gabrain." AU (s.a. 594); "Bass Eoghain maic Gabran." AT 17: 160] Iogenanus is mentioned by Adomnán as a brother of Aidanus, the latter of whom St. Columba at first refused to consecrate as king, because he loved Eóganán more [Adomnán, iii, 5 (p. 189)].

MALE Cuildach mac Gabráin.

MALE Domnall mac Gabráin.

MALE Domangart mac Gabráin.

Gabrán mac Domangairt, King of Dál Riata Male Father: Domangart mac Fergusa, King of Dal Riata ++ [AR7]

Name Gabrán mac Domangairt King of Dál Riata [S1329]

Name [unproved] Gabran King of Dalriada [Gabran the Treacherous]

Name ++ Gabran [AR7]

abt 510 Birth [unproved] Source References: [AR7] Ancestral Roots of Sixty Colonists Who Came To New England before 1700, 7th Ed. [S1329] The Henry Project - Gabrán mac Domangairt Baldwin says his mother is uncertain

Gabrán mac Domangairt, King of Dál Riata and Unknown Children:

Aidan mac Gabran, king of Dalriada (~540-~608) ++ [AR7]

Generation 16 - Domangart mac Fergus or Domangart Reti Of mac Fergus, Rí na Dál Riata

Domangart mac Fergus, was the King of Dalriada from about 501-507, following his father's death. Domangart married Feldem Foltchain, daughter of Brion, son of Eochaid Mugmedon. Brion was an older half -brother of the famous Niall of the Nine Hostages.

Generation 17 - Fergus Mòr Mac Earca or Fergus Mor

The historical record, such as it is, consists of an entry in the Annals of Tigernach, for the year 501, which states: Feargus Mor mac Earca cum gente Dal Riada partem Britaniae tenuit, et ibi mortuus est. (Fergus Mór mac Eirc, with the people of Dál Riata, held part of Britain, and he died there.) However, the forms of Fergus, Erc and Dál Riata are later ones, written down long after the 6th century. The record in the Annals has given rise to theories of invasions of Argyll from Ireland, but these are not considered authentic.[1]

Fergus is also found in the king lists of Dál Riata, and later of Scotland, of which the Senchus Fer n-Alban and the Duan Albanach can be taken as examples. The Senchus states that Fergus Mór was also known as Mac Nisse Mór. These sources probably date from the 10th and 11th centuries respectively, between 30 and 40 generations after Fergus may have lived.

The Senchus and the Duan name Fergus's father as Erc son of Eochaid Muinremuir. A Middle Irish genealogy of the kings of Alba gives an extensive genealogy for Fergus: [Fergus] m. h-Eircc m. Echdach Muinremuir m. Óengusa Fir m. Feideilmid m. Óengusa m. Feideilmid m. Cormaicc, and a further forty-six generations here omitted.[2] While it was suggested some believe Fergus claimed lineage to Arthur, the historian John Morris has suggested, instead, that Fergus was allowed to settle in Scotland as a federate of Arthur, as a bulwark against the Picts.

These sources, while they offer evidence for the importance of Fergus Mór in Medieval times, are not evidence for his historical career. Indeed, only one king in the 6th century in Scotland is known from contemporary evidence, Ceretic of Alt Clut, and even this identification rests upon a later gloss to Saint Patrick's Letter to Coroticus. The first kings of Dál Riata whose existences are reasonably sure are Fergus's grandsons Gabrán mac Domangairt and Comgall, or perhaps his great-grandson Áedán mac Gabráin.

Generation 18 - Erc of Dalriada

Erc was king of Irish Dál Riata until 474. He was the father of Fergus Mór and Loarn mac Eirc, and may have been the great-grandfather of Muirchertach mac Muiredaig. Confusion arises from the latter's matronym, Macc Ercae, said to come from his legendary mother Erca, daughter of Loarn mac Eirc. She married Muiredach mac Eógain. According to the Duan Albanach and the Senchus Fer n-Alban Erc of Dál Riata's father was Eochaid Muinremuir. They may have been descendants of Conaire Cóem.

Suggestions that he was identical with Muiredach mac Eógain and thus belonged to the Uí Néill are based on late sources, such as the Annals of the Four Masters. In fact the Dál Riata are considered Érainn or Darini and claimed to be descendants of the famous Érainn king Conaire Mór. It is typical in late genealogies for unrelated peoples or those only related through marriage to be worked into a single genealogical scheme and all be made descendants of the same legendary founder.

Erc is significant as he has been traditionally regarded as the ancestor, through his son Fergus Mor, of the kings of Dalriada, and through them the Kings of Scotland, but more recently much of this tradition has been questioned.

Generation 19 - Eochaid Muinremuir MAC ÁENGUSA of the Dál-Riata

This is line taken from the Book of Leinster (see CGH p.328-9) and two contemporary pedigrees of William the Lion published in Skene's "Chronicles of the Picts and Scots", considered by Luke Stevens, who has thoroughly compared the various sources, as being probably the most accurate available.

The following is taken from an Internet posting of Michael R. Davidson of Edinburgh. Scotland, on 23 Oct 1995:

II. The Dal Riata and the Pseudo-Historical Section

The Dal Riata, the people from which the Scottish kings are descended, were originally settled on the northeast coast of Ireland. Perhaps as early as the third century, and no later than the fifth century, they began to settle on the west coast of what is now Scotland. It is in the late fifth century that the names in the genealogy begin to take on some historical credibility. In any case, the ruling dynasty of the Dal Riata had established itself in the area corresponding to modern Argyll by the late fifth century. The most important information for this period is the text, probably first written in the seventh century, known as the _Senchus Fer nAlban_, or 'History of the Men of Scotland.' Its early material, however, seems to have far too neat an appearance. Rather than make a fruitless effort to separate fact from fiction, I will instead quote from the _Senchus_, and let the reader come up with their own conclusions. (The genealogies make Eochaid Munremar a son of Oengus Fir, the last name in the above section.)

Two sons of Eochaid Munremar .i. Erc and Olchu. Erc, moreover, had twelve sons .i. six of them took possession of Scotland .i. two Loarnds

.i. Loarnd Bec and Loarnd Mor, two Mac Nisses .i. Mac Nisse Becc and Mac Nisse Mor, two Ferguses .i. Fergus Bec and Fergus Mor. Six others in Ireland .i. Mac Decill, Oengus, whose seed, however, is in Scotland, Enna, Bresal, Fiachra, Dubthach. Others say that this Erc had another son who was called Muredach.

Olchu, son of Eochaid Munremar, had, moreover, eleven sons who live in Murbolc in Dal Riata, Muredach Bolc, Aed, Dare, Oengus, Tuathal, Anbolmaid, Eochaid, Setna, Brian, Oinu, Cormac. (Translation Bannerman)

Generation 20 - Áengus Fert MAC FEIDEILMID

Angus Fir, King of Dalriada

Father: Fedelmid Aislingech, King of Dalriada

Children:

Eochaidh Muinreamhar, King of Dalriada Áengus Fert mac Feideilmid b. circa 350 Father Fedelmid Aislingich mac Áengusa

Áengus Fert mac Feideilmid was born circa 350. He was the son of Fedelmid Aislingich mac Áengusa

Family Child

Eochaid Muinremar mac Áengusa+ b. c 375, d. b 4392

Citations

[S204] Roderick W. Stuart, RfC, 165-54.

[S278] DfAdam, online unknown url, The Line of Fiachu Fer Mara, 109.

[S278] DfAdam, online unknown url, The Line of Fiachu Fer Mara, 108.

Generation 21 - Fedelmid Aislingich MAC ÁENGUSA

Born: Abt 375

Died: Before 439

Fedelmid Aislingich Mac-Aengusa Parents: Aengus Buiding Mac-Feideilmid .

Children were: Angus Fert Mac-Feideilmid.

Generation 22 - Aengus Buiding Mac-Feideilmid

Áengus Buiding mac Feideilmid was the son of Fedelmid Ruamnach mac Senchormac.2 Family Child

Fedelmid Aislingich mac Áengusa+ 1

Citations

[S278] DfAdam, online unknown url, The Line of Fiachu Fer Mara, 107.

[S278] DfAdam, online unknown url, The Line of Fiachu Fer Mara, 106.

Generation 23 - Fedelmid Ruamnach mac Senchormac Fedelmid Ruamnach mac Senchormac was the son of Senchormac mac Cruithluithe.2 Family Child

Áengus Buiding mac Feideilmid+ 1

Citations

[S278] DfAdam, online unknown url, The Line of Fiachu Fer Mara, 106.

[S278] DfAdam, online unknown url, The Line of Fiachu Fer Mara, 105.

Generation 24 - Senchormac mac Cruithluithe Senchormac mac Cruithluithe was the son of Cruithluithe mac Finn Family Child

Fedelmid Ruamnach mac Senchormac+ 1

Citations

[S278] DfAdam, online unknown url, The Line of Fiachu Fer Mara, 105.

[S278] DfAdam, online unknown url, The Line of Fiachu Fer Mara, 104.

Generation 25 - Cruithluithe mac Finn

Cruithluithe mac Finn was the son of Finn Fiacc mac Achir Family Child

Senchormac mac Cruithluithe+ 1

Citations

[S278] DfAdam, online unknown url, The Line of Fiachu Fer Mara, 104.

[S278] DfAdam, online unknown url, The Line of Fiachu Fer Mara, 103.

Generation 26 - Finn Fiacc mac Achir

Finn Fiacc mac Achir was the son of Achir Cirre mac Echach Family Child

Cruithluithe mac Finn+ 1

Citations

[S278] DfAdam, online unknown url, The Line of Fiachu Fer Mara, 103.

[S278] DfAdam, online unknown url, The Line of Fiachu Fer Mara, 102

Generation 27 - Achir Cirre mac Echach

Achir Cirre mac Echach was the son of Eochaid Antóit mac Fiachrach.2 Family Child

Finn Fiacc mac Achir+ 1

Citations

[S278] DfAdam, online unknown url, The Line of Fiachu Fer Mara, 102.

[S278] DfAdam, online unknown url, The Line of Fiachu Fer Mara, 101

Generation 28 - Eochaid Antóit mac Fiachrach

Eochaid Antóit mac Fiachrach was the son of Fiachra Cathmáil mac Echach Family Child

Achir Cirre mac Echach+ 1

Citations

[S278] DfAdam, online unknown url, The Line of Fiachu Fer Mara, 101.

[S278] DfAdam, online unknown url, The Line of Fiachu Fer Mara, 100.

Generation 29 - Fiachra Cathmáil mac Echach

Fiachra Cathmáil mac Echach was the son of Eochaid Riada mac Conaire.2 Family Child

Eochaid Antóit mac Fiachrach+ 1

Citations

[S278] DfAdam, online unknown url, The Line of Fiachu Fer Mara, 100.

[S278] DfAdam, online unknown url, The Line of Fiachu Fer Mara, 99.

Generation 30 - Eochaid Riada mac Conaire

Father Ard-rí na h'Éireann Conaire mac Moga Láma Uí Éremóin3 d. 165 Mother Sarad ingen Conn

Eochaid Riada mac Conaire emigrated first, away from the severe famine in his home of Munster, to the North East of Ireland (Antrim) to found the kingdom of Dal Riata at Ireland. He was born at Munster, Ireland. He ancestor of the Scottish Dal Riada ("a quo Alban Dal Riada"). He was the son of Ard-rí na h'Éireann Conaire mac Moga Láma Uí Éremóin and Sarad ingen Conn. Also called Cairbre Riadal. Eochaid Riada mac Conaire fell out with his followers and crossed the sea, leaving his son behind in fact, to found a second, Scottish, Dal Riata kingdom ("Britain recieved a third nation, that of the Irish, they migrated from Ireland under their chieftain Rueda") in 125 at Scotland. He fought in battle against Dadera, the Druid; Neimhidh, son of Sroibhcinn whom he killed in revenge for his father; and the south of Ireland in 186 at the Battle of Ceannfeabhrat.

Family Child

Fiachra Cathmáil mac Echach

Citations

[S291] Linea Antiqua, online http://members.aol.com/lochlan/clanmac.htm

[S278] DfAdam, online unknown url, The Line of Fiachu Fer Mara, 99.

[S334] Emma Ryan Vol. 1, Myriam Priour Vol. 2 & 3 and Floortje Hondelink Vol. 4, A4M, M165.1.

Generation 31 - Ard-rí na h'Éireann Conaire mac Moga Láma Uí Éremóin Father Mug Láma mac Lugaid Uí Éremóin2 Mother Eithne ingen Lugdach Uí Ítha3

Ard-rí na h'Éireann Conaire mac Moga Láma Uí Éremóin was the son of Mug Láma mac Lugaid Uí Éremóin and Eithne ingen Lugdach Uí Ítha.2,3

Ard-rí na h'Éireann Conaire mac Moga Láma Uí Éremóin was Conaire, son of Modh Lamha.2 Also called Conaire MacMogha Laine.4 He married Sarad ingen Conn, daughter of Conn Cétchathach, Ard-rí na h'Éireann.5 Ard-rí na h'Éireann Conaire mac Moga Láma Uí Éremóin succeeded his 7th cousin, 1x removed, Conn of the Hundred Battles, and ruled his first year over Ireland in 158.2 111th Monarch of Ireland between 158 and 165.2 He died in 165. After having been eight years in the sovereignty of Ireland, fell by Neimhidh, son of Sruibhgheann.5

Family Sarad ingen Conn Children

Eochaid Riada mac Conaire+ 5

Cairbre Baschaein mac Conaire 5

Cairbre Musc mac Conaire 5

Citations

[S278] DfAdam, online unknown url, The Line of Fiachu Fer Mara, 98.

[S334] Emma Ryan Vol. 1, Myriam Priour Vol. 2 & 3 and Floortje Hondelink Vol. 4, A4M, M158.1.

[S278] DfAdam, online unknown url, The Line of Íth mac Breogain, 58.

[S310] John O'Hart, Irish Pedigrees, The Line of Heremon #51, pg. 785.

[S334] Emma Ryan Vol. 1, Myriam Priour Vol. 2 & 3 and Floortje Hondelink Vol. 4, A4M, M165.1.

Generation 32 - Mug Láma mac Lugaid Uí Éremóin

Father Lugaid Allathach mac Cairpre Uí Éremóin2

Mug Láma mac Lugaid Uí Éremóin was the son of Lugaid Allathach mac Cairpre Uí Éremóin.2 Also called Modha Cromcinn.3 Mug Láma mac Lugaid Uí Éremóin married Eithne ingen Lugdach Uí Ítha, daughter of Lugaid mac Dáire Uí Ítha.4

Family Eithne ingen Lugdach Uí Ítha Child

Ard-rí na h'Éireann Conaire mac Moga Láma Uí Éremóin+ d. 1655

Citations

[S278] DfAdam, online unknown url, The Line of Fiachu Fer Mara, 97.

[S278] DfAdam, online unknown url, The Line of Fiachu Fer Mara, 96.

[S310] John O'Hart, Irish Pedigrees, The Line of Heremon #51, pg. 785.

[S278] DfAdam, online unknown url, The Line of Íth mac Breogain, 58.

[S334] Emma Ryan Vol. 1, Myriam Priour Vol. 2 & 3 and Floortje Hondelink Vol. 4, A4M, M158.1.

Generation 33 - Lugaid Allathach mac Cairpre Uí Éremóin Father Cairpre Crommchenn mac Dáire Uí Éremóin

Lugaid Allathach mac Cairpre Uí Éremóin was the son of Cairpre Crommchenn mac Dáire Uí Éremóin.2 Also called Luigheach Allathach.3

Family Child

Mug Láma mac Lugaid Uí Éremóin

Citations

[S278] DfAdam, online unknown url, The Line of Fiachu Fer Mara, 96.

[S278] DfAdam, online unknown url, The Line of Fiachu Fer Mara, 95.

[S310] John O'Hart, Irish Pedigrees, The Line of Heremon #51, pg. 785.

Generation 34 - Cairpre Crommchenn mac Dáire Uí Éremóin Cairpre Crommchenn mac Dáire Uí Éremóin was the son of Dáire Dornmór mac Cairpre Uí Éremóin. Also called Cairbre Cromcinn. Family Child

Lugaid Allathach mac Cairpre Uí Éremóin+ 1

Citations

[S278] DfAdam, online unknown url, The Line of Fiachu Fer Mara, 95.

[S278] DfAdam, online unknown url, The Line of Fiachu Fer Mara, 94.

[S310] John O'Hart, Irish Pedigrees, The Line of Heremon #51, pg. 785.

Generation 35 - Dáire Dornmór mac Cairpre Uí Éremóin or Cairbre Cromcinn

Dáire Dornmór mac Cairpre Uí Éremóin was the son of Cairpre Finn Mór mac Conaire Uí Éremóin.2 Also called Daire Dornmór.3 Family Child

Cairpre Crommchenn mac Dáire Uí Éremóin+ 1

Citations

[S278] DfAdam, online unknown url, The Line of Fiachu Fer Mara, 94.

[S278] DfAdam, online unknown url, The Line of Fiachu Fer Mara, 93.

[S310] John O'Hart, Irish Pedigrees, The Line of Heremon #51, pg. 785.

Generation 36 - Cairpre Finn Mór mac Conaire Uí Éremóin or Cairbre Fionnmór

Cairpre Finn Mór mac Conaire Uí Éremóin was the son of Conaire Mór mac Eterscéoil, Ard-rí na h'Éireann.2 Also called Cairbre Fionnmór.3 Family Child

Dáire Dornmór mac Cairpre Uí Éremóin+ 1

Citations

[S278] DfAdam, online unknown url, The Line of Fiachu Fer Mara, 93.

[S278] DfAdam, online unknown url, The Line of Fiachu Fer Mara, 92.

[S310] John O'Hart, Irish Pedigrees, The Line of Heremon #51, pg. 785

Generation 37 - Conaire Mór mac Eterscéoil, Ard-rí na h'Éireann or Conaire Mór

d. 0040 B.C. Father Eterscél mac Éogan, Ard-rí na h'Éireann1 d. 0110 B.C. Mother Mes Buachalla ingen Echach Uí Éremóin2

Conaire Mór mac Eterscéoil, Ard-rí na h'Éireann died 0040 B.C. At Bruighean Da Dhearg, Ireland. After having been seventy years in the sovereignty of Irelend, was slain by insurgents.1 He ruled his first year over Ireland 0109 B.C..3 97th Monarch of Ireland 0109-0039 B.C..3 He was the son of Eterscél mac Éogan, Ard-rí na h'Éireann and Mes Buachalla ingen Echach Uí Éremóin.1,2 Conaire Mór mac Eterscéoil, Ard-rí na h'Éireann was the son of Ederscel.1,4 Also called Conaire Mór.

Citations

[S334] Emma Ryan Vol. 1, Myriam Priour Vol. 2 & 3 and Floortje Hondelink Vol. 4, A4M, M5160.1.

[S278] DfAdam, online unknown url, The Line of Fiachu Fer Mara, 91.

[S334] Emma Ryan Vol. 1, Myriam Priour Vol. 2 & 3 and Floortje Hondelink Vol. 4, A4M, M5091.1.

[S310] John O'Hart, Irish Pedigrees, The Line of Heremon #40, pg. 785.

[S278] DfAdam, online unknown url, The Line of Fiachu Fer Mara, 92.

Generation 38 - Eterscél mac Éogan, Ard-rí na h'Éireann d. 0110 B.C. Father Éogan mac Ailella Uí Éremóin2

Eterscél mac Éogan, Ard-rí na h'Éireann died 0110 B.C..1 95th Monarch of Ireland 0115-0110 B.C.. He was the son of Éogan mac Ailella Uí Éremóin.2 Also called Edersceal.3 Eterscél mac Éogan, Ard-rí na h'Éireann married Mes Buachalla ingen Echach Uí Éremóin, daughter of Eochaid Airem mac Finn, Ard-rí na h'Éireann and Esa ingen Echach Uí Éremóin.1 Eterscél mac Éogan, Ard-rí na h'Éireann was the father of Conaire Mór mac Eterscéoil, Ard-rí na h'Éireann; the son of Ederscel.4,5

Family Mes Buachalla ingen Echach Uí Éremóin Child

Conaire Mór mac Eterscéoil, Ard-rí na h'Éireann+ d. 0040 B.C.4

Citations

[S278] DfAdam, online unknown url, The Line of Fiachu Fer Mara, 91.

[S278] DfAdam, online unknown url, The Line of Fiachu Fer Mara, 90.

[S310] John O'Hart, Irish Pedigrees, The Line of Heremon #38, pg. 785.

[S334] Emma Ryan Vol. 1, Myriam Priour Vol. 2 & 3 and Floortje Hondelink Vol. 4, A4M, M5160.1.

[S310] John O'Hart, Irish Pedigrees, The Line of Heremon #40, pg. 785.

Generation 39 - Éogan mac Ailella Uí Éremóin

Father Ailill Anglonnach mac Iar Uí Éremóin

Éogan mac Ailella Uí Éremóin was the son of Ailill Anglonnach mac Iar Uí Éremóin.2 Also called Eoghan.3

Family Child

Eterscél mac Éogan, Ard-rí na h'Éireann+ d. 0110 B.C.1

Citations

[S278] DfAdam, online unknown url, The Line of Fiachu Fer Mara, 90.

[S278] DfAdam, online unknown url, The Line of Fiachu Fer Mara, 89.

[S310] John O'Hart, Irish Pedigrees, The Line of Heremon #38, pg. 785.

Generation 40 - Ailill Anglonnach mac Iar Uí Éremóin

Father Iar mac Dedad Uí Éremóin

Ailill Anglonnach mac Iar Uí Éremóin was the son of Iar mac Dedad Uí Éremóin.2 Also called Oilioll.3

Family Child

Éogan mac Ailella Uí Éremóin+ 1

Citations

[S278] DfAdam, online unknown url, The Line of Fiachu Fer Mara, 89.

[S278] DfAdam, online unknown url, The Line of Fiachu Fer Mara, 88.

[S310] John O'Hart, Irish Pedigrees, The Line of Heremon #38, pg. 785.

Generation 41 - Iar mac Dedad Uí Éremóin

Father Dedad mac Sin Uí Éremóin

Iar mac Dedad Uí Éremóin was the son of Dedad mac Sin Uí Éremóin.2 Also called Iar.3

Family Child

Ailill Anglonnach mac Iar Uí Éremóin

Citations

[S278] DfAdam, online unknown url, The Line of Fiachu Fer Mara, 88.

[S278] DfAdam, online unknown url, The Line of Fiachu Fer Mara, 87.

[S310] John O'Hart, Irish Pedigrees, The Line of Heremon #38, pg. 785.

Generation 42 - Dedad mac Sin Uí Éremóin Father Suin mac Roshin Uí Éremóin2

Dedad mac Sin Uí Éremóin was the son of Suin mac Roshin Uí Éremóin.2 Also called Deagha.3

Family Children

Iar mac Dedad Uí Éremóin+ 1

Dáire Donn mac Dedaid Uí Éremóin+ 4

Citations

[S278] DfAdam, online unknown url, The Line of Fiachu Fer Mara, 87.

[S278] DfAdam, online unknown url, The Line of Fiachu Fer Mara, 86.

[S310] John O'Hart, Irish Pedigrees, The Line of Heremon #38, pg. 785.

[S335] Donnchadh Ó Corráin, Rawl. 502, 22].

Generation 43 - Suin mac Roshin Uí Éremóin

Father Roshin mac Trer Uí Éremóin

Suin mac Roshin Uí Éremóin was the son of Roshin mac Trer Uí Éremóin.2 Also called Luin a typo?3

Family Children

Dedad mac Sin Uí Éremóin+ 1

Echdach mac Sin Uí Éremóin+ 2

Citations

[S278] DfAdam, online unknown url, The Line of Fiachu Fer Mara, 86.

[S335] Donnchadh Ó Corráin, Rawl. 502, 1686.

[S310] John O'Hart, Irish Pedigrees, The Line of Heremon #38, pg. 785.

Generation 44 - Roshin mac Trer Uí Éremóin Father Trer mac Rothrer Uí Éremóin2

Roshin mac Trer Uí Éremóin was the son of Trer mac Rothrer Uí Éremóin.2 Also called Roisin.3

Family Child

Suin mac Roshin Uí Éremóin+ 4

Citations

[S278] DfAdam, online unknown url, The Line of Fiachu Fer Mara, 85.

[S278] DfAdam, online unknown url, The Line of Fiachu Fer Mara, 84.

[S310] John O'Hart, Irish Pedigrees, The Line of Heremon #38, pg. 785.

[S335] Donnchadh Ó Corráin, Rawl. 502, 1686.

Generation 45 - Trer mac Rothrer Uí Éremóin

Father Rothrer mac Airndil Uí Éremóin

Trer mac Rothrer Uí Éremóin was the son of Rothrer mac Airndil Uí Éremóin.2 Also called Trein.3

Family Child

Roshin mac Trer Uí Éremóin+ 1

Citations

[S278] DfAdam, online unknown url, The Line of Fiachu Fer Mara, 84.

[S278] DfAdam, online unknown url, The Line of Fiachu Fer Mara, 83.

[S310] John O'Hart, Irish Pedigrees, The Line of Heremon #38, pg. 785.

Generation 46 - Rothrer mac Airndil Uí Éremóin or Trein

Father Rothrer mac Airndil Uí Éremóin2

Trer mac Rothrer Uí Éremóin was the son of Rothrer mac Airndil Uí Éremóin.2 Also called Trein.3

Family Child

Roshin mac Trer Uí Éremóin+ 1

Citations

[S278] DfAdam, online unknown url, The Line of Fiachu Fer Mara, 84.

[S278] DfAdam, online unknown url, The Line of Fiachu Fer Mara, 83.

[S310] John O'Hart, Irish Pedigrees, The Line of Heremon #38, pg. 785.

Generation 47 - Rothrer mac Airndil Uí Éremóin or Rotherein

Father Airndil mac Maine Uí Éremóin2

Rothrer mac Airndil Uí Éremóin was the son of Airndil mac Maine Uí Éremóin.2 Also called Rotherein.3

Family Child

Trer mac Rothrer Uí Éremóin+ 1

Citations

[S278] DfAdam, online unknown url, The Line of Fiachu Fer Mara, 83.

[S278] DfAdam, online unknown url, The Line of Fiachu Fer Mara, 82.

[S310] John O'Hart, Irish Pedigrees, The Line of Heremon #38, pg. 785.

Generation 48 - Airndil mac Maine Uí Éremóin

Father Maine Mór mac Forga Uí Éremóin2

Airndil mac Maine Uí Éremóin was the son of Maine Mór mac Forga Uí Éremóin.2 Also called Airindil.3

Family Child

Rothrer mac Airndil Uí Éremóin+ 1

Citations

[S278] DfAdam, online unknown url, The Line of Fiachu Fer Mara, 82.

[S278] DfAdam, online unknown url, The Line of Fiachu Fer Mara, 81.

[S310] John O'Hart, Irish Pedigrees, The Line of Heremon #38, pg. 785.

RUADRI LINEAGE SOURCES:

The Book of Leinster (Irish Lebor Laignech), is a medieval Irish manuscript compiled ca. 1160 and now kept in Trinity College, Dublin, under the shelfmark MS H 2.18 (cat. 1339). It was formerly known as the Lebor na Nuachongbála "Book of Nuachongbáil", a monastic site known today as Oughaval.

The Martyrology of Tallaght, which is closely related to the Félire Oengusso or Martyrology of Óengus the Culdee, is an eighth- or ninth-century martyrology, a list of saints and their feast days assembled by Máel Ruain and/or Óengus the Culdee at Tallaght Monastery, near Dublin.[1] The Martyrology of Tallaght is in prose and contains two sections for each day of the year, one general and one for Irish saints. It also has a prologue and an epilogue.

The Annals of Ulster (Irish: Annála Uladh) are annals of medieval Ireland. The entries span the years between AD 431 to AD 1540. The entries up to AD 1489 were compiled in the late 15th century by the scribe Ruaidhrí Ó Luinín, under his patron Cathal Óg Mac Maghnusa on the island of Belle Isle on Lough Erne in the province of Ulster. Later entries (up to AD 1540) were added by others.

Previous annals dating as far back as the 6th century were used as a source for the earlier entries, and later entries were based on recollection and oral history. T.M. Charles-Edwards has claimed that the main source for its records of the first millennium AD is a now-lost Armagh continuation of The Chronicle of Ireland. The Annals used the Irish language, with some entries in Latin. Because the Annals copied its sources verbatim, the annals are useful not just for historians, but also for linguists studying the evolution of the Irish language.

A century later, the Annals of Ulster would become an important source for the authors of the Annals of the Four Masters.

The Library of Trinity College Dublin possesses the original manuscript; the Bodleian Library in Oxford has a contemporary copy which fills some of the gaps in the original. There are two main modern English translations of the annals — Mac Airt and Mac Niocaill (1983) and MacCarthy (1893).

Kings of Dál Riata: Alpín Mac Echdach, Áedán Mac Gabráin, List of Kings of Dál Riata, Fergus Mór, Gabrán Mac Domangairt, Comgall Mac Domangairt [Paperback]

Duan Albanach - The Irish version of the Historia Britonum of Nennius (Author: [unknown])

Anderson, Alan Orr, Early Sources of Scottish History A.D 500–1286, volume 1. Reprinted with corrections. Paul Watkins, Stamford, 1990. ISBN 1-871615-03-8

Broun, Dauvit, The Irish Identity of the Kingdom of the Scots in the Twelfth and Thirteenth Centuries. Boydell, Woodbridge, 1999. ISBN 0-85115-375-5

Adomnán, Life of St Columba, tr. & ed. Richard Sharpe. Penguin, London, 1995. ISBN 0-14-044462-9

Lebor Clann Glas

Décès En 560: Clodoald, Chramne, Gabrán Mac Domangairt, Cynric de Wessex (French Edition) [Paperback]

Francis John Byrne, Irish Kings and High-Kings. Four Courts Press. 2nd edition, 2001.

Thomas Charles-Edwards, Early Christian Ireland. Cambridge University Press. 2000.

Donnchadh Ó Corráin (ed.), Genealogies from Rawlinson B 502, at University College Cork: Corpus of Electronic Texts. 1997.

John O'Donovan (ed. and tr.), Annala Rioghachta Eireann. Annals of the Kingdom of Ireland by the Four Masters, from the Earliest Period to the Year 1616. 7 vols. Royal Irish Academy. Dublin. 1848-51. 2nd edition, 1856.

John O'Hart, Irish Pedigrees. Dublin. 5th édition, 1892.

T.F. O'Rahilly, Early Irish History and Mythology. Dublin Institute for Advanced Studies. 1946.

Linea Antiqua, online http://members.aol.com/lochlan/clanmac.htm'''

DfAdam, The Line of Fiachu Fer Mara

Emma Ryan Vol. 1, Myriam Priour Vol. 2 & 3 and Floortje Hondelink Vol. 4, A4M, M165.1

Donnchadh Ó Corráin, Rawl. 502, 22

————————————————————————————Other notes:

From: http://fmg.ac/Projects/MedLands/SCOTLAND.htm

Malcolm I had [one illegitimate child by an unknown mistress]:

3. [KENNETH . The Chronicle of John of Fordun records that "Constantine the Bald, son of King Culen" succeeded in 994 after King Kenneth II was killed, but that he was "continually harassed by Malcolm [son of King Kenneth] and his illegitimate uncle…Kenneth" and killed in battle "in Laudonia by the banks of the river Almond" after reigning for one and a half years[184]. He is not mentioned in any of the earlier sources so far consulted. His existence should be treated with caution.]

[DONADA . Many secondary sources name Donada as a younger daughter of King Malcolm II and the mother of King Macbeth. It seems that the proof for this connection is slim. The only source so far identified which refers to Macbeth´s maternal origin is the Chronicle of Huntingdon which names "Maket Regem [=King Macbeth] nepotem dicti Malcolmi" when recording that he was expelled from Scotland after ruling 15 years. The word "nepos" is of course treacherous and could indicate a variety of relationships in addition to grandson. However, it appears that early historians assumed that "grandson" was the correct translation. For example, Ralph Holinshed´s 1577 Chronicle of Scotland names "Doada" as second daughter of Malcolm II King of Scotland and adds that she married "Sinell the thane of Glammis, by whom she had issue one Makbeth"[176]. Another variation is provided by the Cronykil of

Andrew of Wyntoun, which records that "Makbeth-Fynlak, his systyr sowne" murdered King Duncan. From a chronological point of view, it is unlikely that Macbeth could have been a nephew of King Duncan, but it is possible that the passage represents an interpretation of "nepos" from an earlier source and has confused the king with whom Macbeth enjoyed this relationship. No source earlier than Holinshed has been found which names her Donada. m as his second wife, FINDLAECH MacRory Thane of Angus Mormaer of Moray, son of RUAIDHRI Mormaer of Moray & his wife -—(-1020). The Annals of Ulster record the death in 1020 of "Finnlaech son of Ruadrí king of Alba...killed by his own people".

Máel Coluim mac Domnaill (anglicised Malcolm I)

Máel Coluim mac Cináeda (Modern Gaelic: Maol Chaluim mac Choinnich,[1] known in modern anglicized regnal lists as Malcolm II; died 25 November 1034

Cináed mac Maíl Coluim (Modern Gaelic: Coinneach mac Mhaoil Chaluim[1] anglicised as Kenneth II

http://en.wikipedia.org/wiki/User:Deacon_of_Pndapetzim/Kings

Máel Coluim of Moray (or Máel Coluim mac Máil Brigti) was King or Mormaer of Moray (1020–1029), and, as his name suggests, the son of a Máel Brigte. As with his predecessor Findláech mac Ruaidrí, sources call him "King of Scotland."

Rather confusingly for some of our sources and for some historians, Máel Coluim held the kingship contemporaneously with another Máel Coluim, Máel Coluim II (mac Cináeda) of Scotland. The Orkneyinga Saga for instance tells us that Thorfinn Sigurdsson, Earl of Orkney was the son of the daughter of Máel Coluim, king of Scotland. Some historians have argued that this was Máel Coluim mac Cináeda of Scotland, but Hudson has suggested that Máel Coluim mac Máil Brigti is the more likely candidate (p. 135).

His death date derives from the Annals of Tigernach, which notes s.a. 1029, "Mael Colaim mac Mael-Brighdi mac Ruaidrí, rí Alban mortuus est (="Máel

Coluim, son of Máel Brigte, son of Ruadrí, King of Scotland, dies")." As can be seen, if it were not for the mac Mael-Brighdi, we could easily assume we were being given an inaccurate date for the death of King Máel Coluim II.

Máel Coluim mac Máil Brigti seems to have been succeeded by his brother Gille Coemgáin.

Domnall mac Máil Coluim, "son of the King of Scotland", whose death is reported by the Annals of Ulster s.a. 1085, may have been a son of this Máel Coluim, or perhaps of Máel Coluim mac Donnchada (Malcolm III). http://en.wikipedia.org/wiki/M%C3%A1el_Coluim_of_Moray

Findláech of Moray, or Findláech mac Ruaidrí, was the King or Mormaer of Moray, ruling from some point before 1014 until his death in 1020. In the Annals of Ulster and in the Book of Leinster, Findláech is called rí Alban, which meant "King of Scotland" in the Gaelic language. As far as we know from other sources, the only rí Alban of the time was Máel Coluim mac Cináeda, i.e. Máel Coluim II, so this title can only mean that Findláech, as ruler of Moray, was understood by many to have been the High-King of all northern Britain. However, Findláech's main claim to fame these days is as the father of Mac Bethad, made famous by William Shakespeare's play Macbeth. Indeed, the Irish historian known in Latin as Marianus Scotus calls Macbethad simply MacFindlaeg. Historians are fairly certain that Findláech was ruling before 1014 because the Orkneyinga Saga reads that before the Battle of Clontarf, Jarl Siguðr of Orkney fought a battle with the Scots, who were led by a Jarl Finnlekr (i.e. Findláech the Mormaer). An Irish princess called Eithne made a banner for Siguðr, which had on it a raven. The saga records that Siguðr later brought the banner to Clontarf, where he was killed. If we believe this, then Findláech would be ruler quite a bit before 1014. His death date, as mentioned above, derives from the Annals of Ulster, which notes s.a. 1020 Finnloech m. Ruaidhri, ri Alban, a suis occisus est, that is, that Findláech was killed by his own people. No reason for this is given, but the logical thing is to conclude that his successor, his nephew Máel Coluim mac Máil Brigti, had something to do with it. Indeed, the Annals of Tigernach tell us that the sons of Máel Brigte were responsible; the only sons we know of are Máel Coluim and

Gille Coemgáin, both of whom evidently benefited from the killing, as both succeeded to the throne.

http://www.euppublishing.com/doi/abs/10.3366/shr.2000.79.2.145

The Scottish Historical Review is the premier journal in the field of Scottish Historical Studies, covering all periods of Scottish history from the early to the modern, encouraging a variety of historical approaches.

Below is as written by author Frank O'Collins) -

Mac Bethad mac Findlaích was born to King Findláech mac Ruadrí of Moray—of the legendary Kings of Dál Riata and later Alba (Scotland)—the "Holly"

(Cuilliaéan) druid priest kings originally from Ireland and Fergus Mor in the 8th Century. In 997, Holly King Causantín mac Cuiléain of Alba (Scotland) was murdered by Cináed mac Ailpín (Kenneth MacAlpin) of the treacherous Uí Néill declaring himself the new King. Later, the origin of Kenneth MacAlpin was deliberately corrupted by "writer for hire" John of Fordun who in the 14th Century was paid handsomely by King Edward III to destroy the true history of Scotland and Ireland and write a wholly ficticious tale.

After the historic coup, the last remaining Holly bloodline and rightful heir to the throne of Scotland was the younger brother of Causantín, King Ruadrí of Moray. When "King" Kenneth was killed at the battle of Clontarf in 1005, his son Máel Coluim mac Cináeda (Malcolm the destroyer) took the throne. His first act as King was to invite King Ruadrí of Moray to discuss terms of a peace treaty, at which King Malcolm broke his solemn oath as a King and had King Ruadrí murdered. King Ruadrí was then succeeded by his son Findláech mac Ruadrí as King of Moray.

The continuing treachery of the Uí Néill usurpers to the throne of Scotland plunged the whole region into civil war for thirty years, during which Malcolm succeeded in destroying virtually every major landmark, building, church, school, monastery, and asset of Scotland—hence his historic name. By 1032, he finally achieved his aim in killing King Findláech mac Ruadrí of Moray in 1032—the father of Macbeth.

In 1034, King Malcolm the destroyer finally died and was succeeded by his son Donnchad mac Crínáin also known as Duncan as King of Alba (Scotland). In 1039, Duncan planned one final push to invade the kingdom of Moray and eliminate Macbeth and the last of the Holly. However, at the battle of Pitgaveny near Elgin, upon the orders by Duncan for his troops to attack Macbeth full-frontal, his troops rebelled and killed the King. Thus in 1039, Macbeth became the last Holly King of Scotland.

Unfortunately, the infant son of Duncan, whose name was Máel Coluim mac Donnchad (Malcolm the Traitor) escaped with his family to Northumbria and the court of Siward the Dane. Siward then raised him as his own son, even granting him the title of King of Strathclyde.

When Siward the Dane died in 1055, Malcolm, the son of Duncan and Earl of Northumbria took his army northward to confront Macbeth but was badly beaten. Upon his return to Northumbria, Malcolm was then humiliated in being stripped of his inheritance by King Edward the Confessor (1042-1066) who then appointed Tostig Godwinson as the new Earl.

Malcolm made a desperate appeal to Edward the Confessor for troops, including his oath and loyalty as a vassal of England—effectively selling Scotland to the House of Wessex to regain the crown. With that deal, Edward provided Malcolm with a large mercenary army which invaded Scotland in 1058.

Heavily outnumbered, Macbeth held Malcolm's forces at the north side of the Mounth but was forced to retreat over the Cairnamounth Pass where at the battle of Lumphanan Macbeth was severley wounded. Malcolm mistakenly believed that Macbeth had been taken back to his family castle at Dunsinane Hill and ordered it destroyed, killing the entire Macbeth clan. Instead, Macbeth was taken to Scone, where he died in 1058—the last Holly king of Scotland."

From "Labor Clan Glas" -

Home Scripture Book Index < Previous Next > you are here: > The Book of the Clann Glas (Green Race) > Chapter 27

Chapter 27 - 904 CE

563. 1. From the year 904 2. Since the birth of John the Baptist (904 AD) 3. A Sadducee House of unheralded evil 4. known as the counts of Tusculum 5. did seize the Papacy and political power 6. First through Pope Sergius III 7. a man of unprecedented evil 8. For he introduced a tradition to the Popes 9. that they would not only father 10. illegitimate children as almost all Popes 11. had done for generations 12. but that the Popes would commit incest 13. with their own children 14. in order to produce more Popes 15. Further that those children not favoured 16. would be used for great ceremonies 17. of human sacrifice in honor of the demonic gods 18. of the Sadducee jews 19. So it was that Pope Sergius III 20. did commit incest with his daughter Marozie 21. who he made his mistress 22. and their son then 23. became Pope John X 24. also known as Pope John XI, Pope John XII 25. and Pope John XIII to hide the fact 26. of his great reign as Supreme Pontiff of the Catholic Church 27. But the reign of Pope Sergius III 28. was nothing to compare to the Papacy of his son 29. A rule of over 37 years across at least four papacy's 30. For upon his first papacy 31. he converted all the convents of Rome into brothels 32. he openly participated in satanic masses in daylight 33. murdering countless innocent victims 34. Pope John did also take his mother Marozie 35. to be his mistress and wife 36. and even fathered several children 37. with his mother 38. Except for the city wide orgies of the Borgia Popes 39. in many years to come 40. Rome has never seen the rivers of blood 41. nor pure evil as the reign of the House of Tusculum 42. for over 100 years 564. 1. In the year 943 2. Since the birth of John the Baptist (943 AD) 3. Holly King Causantín mac Áeda 4. Son of Áeda mac Causantín 5. grandson of Causantín mac Domnall 6. great grandson of Domnall mac Causantín 7. great great grandson of Caustantín mac Fergusa 8.

three times great grandson of Fergus mac Echdach 9. four times great grandson of Eochaid mac Echdach 10. five times great grandson of Eochaid mac Domangart 11. six times great grandson of Domangart mac Domnall 12. seven times great grandson of Domnall mac Echdach 13. eight times great grandson of Son of Eochaid mac Áedán 14. nine times great grandson of Áedán mac Gabráin 15. ten times great grandson of Gabrán mac Domangairt 16. eleven times great grandson of Domangart mac Fergus 17. twelve times great grandson of Fergus Mor 18. Descendent of the most ancient Holly druids 19. Descendent of the High Kings of Ireland 20. Did give up the ghost 21. The kingship of Alba (Scotland) then did fall 22. to his son Ildulb mac Causantín 23. the sixth king of united Scotland 565. 1. In the year 962 2. Since the birth of John the Baptist (962AD) 3. Holly King Ildulb mac Causantín 4. Son of Causantín mac Áeda 5. grandson of Áeda mac Causantín 6. great grandson of Causantín mac Domnall 7. great great grandson of Domnall mac Causantín 8. three times great grandson of Caustantín mac Fergusa 9. four times great grandson of Fergus mac Echdach 10. five times great grandson of Eochaid mac Echdach 11. six times great grandson of Eochaid mac Domangart 12. seven times great grandson of Domangart mac Domnall 13. eight times great grandson of Domnall mac Echdach 14. nine times great grandson of Son of Eochaid mac Áedán 15. ten times great grandson of Áedán mac Gabráin 16. eleven times great grandson of Gabrán mac Domangairt 17. twelve times great grandson of Domangart mac Fergus 18. thirteen times great grandson of Fergus Mor 19. Descendent of the most ancient Holly druids 20. Descendent of the High Kings of Ireland 21. Did give up the ghost 22. The kingship of Alba (Scotland) then did fall 23. to his son Cuiléain mac Iduilb 24. whose name means Holly 25. the seventh king of united Scotland 566. 1. In the year 971 2. Since the birth of John the Baptist (971 AD) 3. Holly King Cuiléin mac Iduilb 4. Son of Ildulb mac Causantín 5. grandson of Causantín mac Áeda 6. great grandson of Áeda mac Causantín 7. great great grandson of Causantín mac Domnall 8. three times great grandson of Domnall mac Causantín 9. four times great grandson of Caustantín mac Fergusa 10. five times great grandson of Fergus mac Echdach 11. six times great grandson of Eochaid mac Echdach 12. seven times great grandson of Eochaid mac Domangart 13. eight times great grandson of Domangart mac Domnall 14. nine times great grandson of Domnall mac Echdach 15. ten times great grandson of Son of Eochaid mac Áedán 16. eleven times great grandson of Áedán mac Gabráin 17. twelve times great grandson of Gabrán mac Domangairt 18. thirteen times great grandson of Domangart mac Fergus 19. fourteen times great grandson of Fergus Mor 20. Descendent of the most ancient Holly druids 21. Descendent of the High Kings of Ireland 22. Did give up the ghost 23. The kingship of Alba (Scotland) then did fall 24. to his son Causantín mac Cuiléain 25. known as the true Constantine IV 26. the eighth king of united Scotland 567. 1. In the year 997 2. Since the birth of John the Baptist (997 AD) 3. Holly King Causantín mac Cuiléain 4. Son of Cuiléain mac Iduilb 5. grandson of Ildulb mac Causantín 6. great grandson of Causantín mac Áeda 7. great great grandson of Áeda mac Causantín 8. three times great grandson of Causantín mac Domnall 9. four times great grandson of Domnall mac Causantín 10. five times great grandson of Caustantín mac Fergusa 11. six times great grandson of Fergus mac Echdach 12. seven times great grandson of Eochaid mac Echdach 13. eight times great grandson of Eochaid mac Domangart 14. nine times great grandson of Domangart mac Domnall 15. ten times great grandson of Domnall mac Echdach 16. eleven times great grandson of Son of Eochaid mac Áedán 17. twelve times great grandson of Áedán mac Gabráin 18. thirteen times great grandson of Gabrán mac Domangairt 19. fourteen times great grandson of Domangart mac Fergus 20. fifteen times great grandson of Fergus Mor 21. Descendent of the most ancient Holly druids 22. Descendent of the High Kings of Ireland 23. Was murdered by the commander of the Royal guard 24. Known as Cináed mac Ailpín 25. And as Kenneth the Brown 26. And as Kenneth MacAlpin 27. wrongly re-written as Cináed mac Duib 28. by artificer of the pen John of Fordun 29. to hide the truth of his clan of assassins 30. most spineless and treacherous 31. changed of name to hide his evil deed 32. Formed the House of Alpin 33. falsely known as the House of Dunkeld 34. on account of his grandson 35. upon murdering the Holly High King 36.

and his whole family 37. Kenneth MacAlpin did claim 38. The sons of the Holly King 39. Did kill their father and Kenneth 40. Did slay them as assassins 41. Inheriting the crown upon his adoption 42. As a son of the King 43. And his dying wish 44. Many of the cousins of the Holly King 45. Did protest such claims as clearly false 46. Ruadrí of Moray 47. the younger brother of The slain King Constantine 48. Did protest loudly 49. At the falseness of these claims 50. But too powerful was MacAlpin 51. On account of the alliances 52. He had made with Uí Néill king 53. Máel Sechnaill mac Domnaill 54. Of the Clann Cholmáin of the southern Uí Néill Of Ireland 55. a relative of Kenneth MacAlpin 56. And alliances for troops 57. with Waltheof the King of Bernicia and Earl of Northumbria 58. Kenneth MacAlpin the assassin 59. Was a crafty king 60. And upon being crowned 61. upon The white (limestone) stone of destiny 62. And the Marble throne of Amen-Ra 63. King Kenneth did claim the ancient right 64. Of the lands to the north of Ireland 65. As being the Kingdom of Alba 66. On account of them once being part of Dál Riata 67. Calling himself Emperor of the Celtic Tribes 68. The northern Uí Néill did reject his claim 69. And King Kenneth MacAlpin 70. Did invade the north of Ireland 71. In the year 1005 72. And the Battle of Clontarf did ensue 73. At which King Kenneth was killed 74. Later to be reborn as Brian Boru 75. Through the creative lies 76. Of the Uí Brian 77. To claim kingship 568. 1. In the year 1005 2. Since the birth of John the Baptist (1005 AD) 3. Cináed mac Ailpín the assassin 4. Known as King Kenneth MacAlpin 5. Was succeeded by his son 6. Máel Coluim mac Cináeda 7. known as Malcolm the destroyer 8. A bloodthirsty tyrant was Malcolm 9. And set about killing all the Holly family 10. He could find 11. enslaving the Scots 12. and taxing all merchants as much as he could 13. Within his first year he succeeded 14. In killing Ruadrí of Moray 15. the younger brother of the slain King Constantine 16. But his family escaped 17. And Malcolm turned his attention 18. To building alliances for his own greatness 19. Malcolm did go to Rome 20. And even to England 21. And in 1032 Malcolm 22. Did kill Findláech mac Ruadrí 23. The King of Moray 24. And rightful heir of the throne of Alba (Scotland) 25. Yet himself did die two years later (1034) 569. 1. In the year 1032

2. Since the birth of John the Baptist (1032 AD) 3. And the murder of Findláech mac Ruadrí 4. The true King of Alba (Scotland) 5. By Malcolm of the House of Assassins 6. Known as Alpin 7. His son known as Mac Bethad mac Findláích 8. Whose name was MacBeth 9. Of the fame of stories and legends 10. But was the true Heir to the Kingship of Alba (Scotland) 11. On account of being of the Holly family 12. The Cuileain and Cuilleain 13. The most ancient druids and High Kings of Ireland 14. Descendents of the greatest prophets and kings 15. Did become King of Moray 16. MacBeth was a mighty warrior 17. And wise king 18. Who earned the name Rí Deircc 19. Which means the Red King 20. While he longed for the day to avenge 21. The murder of his family 22. By one of the most treacherous families 23. To ever walk the sacred earth of Scotland 24. He was wise to wait for the right opportunity 25. Lest the alliance of the House of Alpin 26. Bring great war upon the land 570. 1. In the year 1034 2. Since the birth of John the Baptist (1034 AD) 3. The son of Malcolm 4. And grandson of Kenneth MacAlpin 5. Whose name was Donnchad mac Crínáin 6. Also known as Duncan 7. Did become King of Alba 8. A poor general of men 9. Who inherited all the wickedness of his father 10. Hated by all of Scotland 11. On account of his cruel murder of many scholars 12. of priests and innocent people 13. And those that would not worship him as a great king 14. In the year 1039 15. Duncan decided he would invade the lands of Moray 16. And kill MacBeth and all the remainder of his clan 17. So no more contest would there be 18. against the house of treachery 19. The house of Alpin and Dunkeld 20. But MacBeth was a greater match for Duncan 21. And the troops of Duncan did suffer great losses 22. Upon a battle at Pitgaveny near Elgin 23. Upon the order of the mad King Duncan 24. That his troops attack full frontal upon MacBeth 25. His own troops did kill the King 26. And surrender to MacBeth 27. Recognizing his legal right and Kingship 28. Thus in the year 1039 29. MacBeth became the last Holly King 30. To rule Scotland 31. The very last Holly King 32. of all history 571. 1. In the year 1039 2. Since the birth of John the Baptist (1039 AD) 3. At the royal court in Scone 4. King MacBeth was the last Holly King 5. And the last King on either British or Irish soil 6. To be anointed upon the true 7. White (limestone) Stone of Destiny 8. And to sit upon the Green Marble Throne of Amen-Ra 9. King MacBeth showed himself as wise a king 10. As any of the Great Holly High Kings 11. Of ages past 12. Upon the wars between the English Earls and Kings 13. He accepted Norman exiles into his court 14. Treating all with respect and justice 15. He restored the rights of laws of the land 16. So wickedly taken by the House of Alpin 17. And increased trade with all 18. But Máel Coluim mac Donnchada 19. Also known as Malcolm 20. The infant son of Duncan who was slain by own troops 21. Did escape with some of his household 22. To Northumbria and the court of Siward the Dane 23. Who did raise Malcolm the son of Duncan 24. As his own 25. And when he was of age, he was granted the title 26. Of King of Strathclyde 27. By his adopted father 572. 1. In the year 1055 2. Since the birth of John the Baptist (1055 AD) 3. Upon the death of Siward the Dane 4. The Earl of Northumbria 5. Malcolm, the son of Duncan 6. Did take the army northwards 7. And confront King MacBeth 8. MacBeth was a superior commander 9. And held his ground against the superior numbers 10. Of the Northumbrians 11. But did encounter heavy losses 12. as fate would have it 13. The commanders of the Northumbrians 14. Were called to withdraw 15. By the English crown 16. As a new Earl of Northumbria 17. Whose name was Tostig Godwinson 18. Did the English appoint 19. And the invasion was abandoned 20. Malcolm did go to England 21. To make his case against MacBeth 22. It is here that he did speak such vile lies 23. And wicked untruth concerning 24. King MacBeth 25. by using the true evil of his own ancestry 26. And claiming it as MacBeth 27. Upon hearing of such trickery 28. And wishing a strong ally in the Scots 29. The English did supply the traitor 30. And liar Malcolm with a new army 31. With which to defeat MacBeth 573. 1. In the year 1057 2. Since the birth of John the Baptist (1057 AD) 3. King MacBeth did receive word 4. That Malcolm the traitor of Scotland 5. From the House of Assassins 6. The House of Alpin 7. was approaching with a massive army 8. As MacBeth prepared his battled plans 9. An old woman from the far North 10. Known to be a prophetess 11. Did come to MacBeth 12. And foretold of his defeat 13. And the end of the line of the Holly Kings 14. That he must save the ancient relics 15. From falling into the hands of the traitor Malcolm 16. For surely they would then be given to the English 17. And with such symbols of power 18. The English could wage great evil and war 19. So MacBeth ordered his most trusted troops 20. To take the Stony of destiny 21. The Marble Throne of Amen-Ra 22. The round tables of Cormac Mac Art 23. the Standard of the House of Judah 24. and other most ancient relics 25. and buried them deeply 26. near his ancestral home 27. the castle of Dunsinane Hill 28. in the lands of Perthshire 574. 1. In the year 1058 2. Since the birth of John the Baptist (1058 AD) 3. Malcolm and his mercenary army 4. Did invade Scotland 5. And Macbeth valiantly held the forces at bay 6. At the north side of the Mounth 7. But heavily outnumbered he retreated 8. over the Cairnamounth Pass 9. and his last battle Lumphanan 10. wounded and defeated his guard 11. took him from the battlefield 12. Malcolm believed MacBeth had been taken 13. To his fort at Dunsinane Hill 14. And ordered it destroyed 15. Killing the family of MacBeth 16. And his heirs 17. Instead, MacBeth was taken to Scone 18. as was prophesized 19. and the good king died 20. Malcom triumphant through his treachery 21. And treason against the honor of Scotland 22. Then proclaimed himself king 23. But upon finding the most sacred artifacts 24. And no one alive to torture as to their location 25. He cursed the name MacBeth 26. And try as he might 27. as did his descendants 28. None did find the location of the true relics 29. For eight hundred more years 30. The Last Holly King was dead 31. A legend begun from the beginning of time 32. Was gone forever 575. 1. In the year 1099 2. Since the birth of John the Baptist (1099 AD) 3. Christian Knights, priests 4. and members of the first crusade 5. slaughtered every single man, woman, child 6. and animal in Jerusalem, 7. sparing not one soul 8. upon the specific and clear orders 9. of Blessed Pope Urban II 10. Over two hundred thousand souls died 11. by the order of the Pope 12. sixty thousand of which were Jewish 13. But on account they were not Sadducee jews 14. of noble blood, not one was spared. 576. 1. In the year 1102 2. Since the birth of John the Baptist (1102 AD) 3. Magnus III of Norway 4. invaded Ireland and captured Dublin. 5. the city rebuilt by his ancestors 6. Yet his stay and life in Ireland was short lived 7. for the following year (1103) 8. Muircheartach Ua Briain 9. a thoroughly wicked and immoral leader 10. had him assassinated 11. by dressing up some of his men as priests 12. at Downpatrick, County Down 13. In the year 1104 14. Muircheartach Ua Briain 15. did commission the first of three horrendous frauds 16. all designed to strengthen his claim of Kingship 17. and secure the claims of his heirs 18. The first was a heavily doctored version of Táin Bó Cúailnge 19. the foundation story of the Ulster Epic 20. originally commissioned by Cormac Mac Art 21. over eight hundreds years prior 22. but now resembling it only in name 23. within the publication Lebor na hUidre 24. which means Book of the Dun Cow 25. by the Christian monastery of Clonmacnoise 26. in exchange for a handsome bribe 27. The second great forgery was the work called 28. Cogadh Gaedhil re Gallaibh 29. The War of the Irish with the Foreigners 30. by Muirchertach Ua Briain 31. In which a completely fabled king called Brian Boru 32. was supposed to be the founder of the clan 33. The truth of Thomond long buried 34. The truth of the Ua Briain history as petty mercenaries 35. from foreign lands 36. long written out of a new history which they created 37. The third and final fraudulent epic 38. created by Muirchertach Ua Briain 39. was called Brjánssaga 40. which means Brjáns saga 41. Yet another story of mythical heroes 42. from which the Ua Briain were supposed to have risen 43. Not as paid mercenaries who came in search 44. of gold and plunder during the first invasions 45. of Papal forces in the year 430 577. 1. In the year 1119 2. Since the birth of John the Baptist (1119 AD) 3. Two veteran French knights from the first crusade 4. whose names were Hugues de Payens and Godfrey de Saint-Omer 5. came into the possession 6. of a most ancient letter 7. from the time of the House of Ananias 8. Upon request The two knights 9. did receive permission 10. by Baldwin II of Jerusalem 11. to establish a monastic order 12. for the protection of pilgrims 13. and specifically requested the vacant Temple Mount site 14. The king agreed and the order was formed under the title 15. Poor Knights of Christ and the Temple of Solomon 16. or Templar Knights 17. But for the first eight years 18. the Templars did nothing but dig 19. and around the maze *of caves and catacombs 20. that exist within the base of the Temple Mount 21. Then in the year 1128 22. The two men discovered 23. a most ancient and preserved head 24. hidden in a clay jar 25. They went on to call this head 26. The Baphomet 27. The wise head 28. Also known as the head of prophecy 29. It being the severed head 30. of Jesus known as Christ 31. which Paul of Tarsus cut off 32. when he murdered him in France 33. bringing the head to the High priests 34. who in turn hid it within the bowels of the Temple 35. Within one year of their discovery 36. The Templars had the patronage of Bernard of Clairvaux 37. one of the wealthiest men 38. and official recognition by the church 39. Within ten more years (1139) 40. Pope Innocent II with a papal bull 41. named Omne Datum Optimum 42. exempted the Order from obedience to local laws. 43. Thus the Templars for two hundred years 44. became the most powerful and mysterious order 45. to ever exist within the Catholic Church 46. Yet upon their disbandment 47. The Baphomet was never found 48. Nor were the secret documents found 49. at the same time 50. The location of the Templar Treasure 51. being these things has remained a mystery 578. 1. In the year 1151 2. Since the birth of John the Baptist (1151 AD) 3. Pope Eugine III did commission 4. a master forger named Gratian 5. to create a supremely false document 6. called the Decretum 7. using cleaned and ancient parchments 8. incorporating the forged Isidorian Decretals 9. then combined with two other major forgeries 10. The Donation of Constantine 11. and the Liber Pontificalis 12. along with other falsified writings 13. and codified into a system of Church law 14. which elevated Gregory 15. and all his successors as absolute monarchs 16. claiming supremecy of the world 579. 1. In the year 1154 2. Since the birth of John the Baptist (1154 AD) 3. King Henry II of England 4. Did undertake a plan that would once and for all 4. Destroy the sacred soul of Ireland 4. And render it a broken vassal of England 4. First, he did address the seizure 4. of the sacredness of Ireland 4. King Henry II commissioned Geoffrey of Monmouth 5. and a team of founding scholars 6. granted to form Oxford University 7. To produce a wholly fraudulent work 8. called Historia Regum Britanniae 9. History of the Kings of Britain 10. wholly stolen from real Irish history 11. to eliminate all real Irish history 12. by assigning it to England 13. a strategy that largely succeeded 14. for over 900 years 15. Second, King Henry II 16. undertook an agreement with Pope Adrian IV 17. whereby the Pope issued a Papal Bull 18. One of the most evil documents of history 19. called Laudabiliter 20. which was doctored in later centuries 21. to hide its real contents 22. For in 1155 this claim of the Pope 23. Based on all the forgeries of the past Popes 24. was that the Vatican legally owned Ireland 25. including its people 26. So Pope Adrian IV did then sell Ireland 27. and all the Irish as slaves 28. to King Henry II of England 29. in exchange for a handsome annual sum 30. a tribute of supreme evil 31. only ended under the reign of another Henry 32. with many wives 33. The truth that the Vatican was paid by England 34. The fact that the Popes sold the Irish nation 35. as slaves now disputed 36. by yet more frauds and lies 580. 1. In the year 1158 2. Since the birth of John the Baptist (1158 AD) 3. King Henry II of England 4. Did continue his rape of the soul of Ireland 5. By stealing the official standard 6. of the cuilleain the Holly 7. as last remaining bloodline of House of Judah 8. the lion rampant 9. A symbolizm of his claim over Ireland 10. And the former Holly kingdom of Scotland 11. But in colour reverse did the King order it 12. a golden lion on a red field 13. a theft of historic proportions 14. that has held for far too long 15. No right to the lion did England have 16. Nor has England ever had 17. Other than pillagers, brigands and assassins 581. 1. In the year 1169 2. Since the birth of John the Baptist (1169 AD) 3. The Army of King Henry II 4. did land in Wexford 5. and crush the Irish forces 6. on request of deposed High King 7. and traitor Diarmuid MacMorrough 8. Upon regaining High Kingship 9. using Henry's forces 10. The great traitor of Ireland 11. Diarmuid MacMorrough 12. did then switch sides again 13. nominating his own son as successor 14. In the year 1170 15. King Henry II 16. did send his most cruel and evil general 17. whose name was Richard de Clare 18. also known as Strongbow 19. In the following year (1171) 20. King Henry II sent an even larger army 21. that landed at Waterford 22. The first English King 23. to ever set foot on Irish soil. 24. Henry did then make Strongbow King of Leinster 25. Upon being made a King 26. Strongbow ordered the complete dismantling of Tara 27. That no memory be left, not one stone 28. Thus a force of several thousand Englishman 29. using Irish as slaves 30. Forced the removal of millions of stones 31. of countless beams of wood 32. The stones then used for Norman forts 33. Until all that was left of Tara 34. was a hill of dirt 35. soon to be fields 36. As if it had never existed 37. Thus the damnation of Ireland was complete 38. Its history stolen 39. The truth turned to myth 40. Its people enslaved by the church the followed 41. Captive to a force that hated them with every fibre 42. Every book of its history 43. Burnt or corrupted beyond recognition 44. Every ancient road torn up 45. Every ancient school destroyed 582. 1. But for one thing Ireland did survive 2. Not for lost history 3. Nor for ancient Kingship 4. The memory of greatness 5. It was the most precious thing 6. The one thing that could not be stolen 7. The spirit, the soul 8. that dwells in all Irish 9. the same spirit that enlightened the world 10. the same spirit that saved the world 11. many times over 12. a spirit that is called again 13. as darkness and resolution approach 14. first priest first king 15. the green race.*

The above taken from the Islamic Scriptures "Lebor Clan Glass"

Bibliography

"*Thanks go to Virginia C. HANKS for providing a copy of Carrie Alexander WOOD's genealogy, which she obtained from WOOD's niece, Carolyn SYSKA. WOOD quotes the following sources for her work: The Chart of Descent of House of FINLEY, from Manuscript Pedigrees at the Society of Genealogy, London, derived from Annals of Four Masters, CONNELLY's Irish Families and KEATING's History of Ireland.*"

History of Ireland, by Standish O'GRADY.

History of Ireland, by Thomas WRIGHT.

History of Ireland, by Thomas MOORE.

Annals of Ulster. Irish Antiquarean Research.

History of Scotland, by John Hill BURTON.

Lands and Their Owners, by P.H. MC KERLIE, Scotland.

Prehistoric Annals, by Daniel WILSON.

Isle of Bute, by James King HEWESON.

Celtic Scotland, by William F. SKINE.

The Highland Clans, by EYRE.

Clans, Septs and Regiments of the Scottish Highlands, by Frank ADAM.

Their Majesties of Scotland, by E. Thornton COOK.

Wynton's Annals<.

Cupar Angus Cistereian Abbey.

Register of St. Andrew's Parish, Fifeshire, Scotland.

House of FINLEY Castle Toward, by George FINLEY, LLD.

House of FINLEY, by the Rev. John Borland FINLEY.

Various Presbyterian parish records of Scotland.

Various Presbyterian parish records of Ireland.

Encyclopedia Brittanica.

Pennsylvania Magazine of History and Biography.

Prerogative Wills, Scotland and Ireland.

Presbytery of New Castle, DE.

Pennsylvania Archives.

Scotch-Irish in Cumberland Co, PA.

Virginia wills and deeds.

CHALKEY's Augusta County Records, Vols. 1-3.

History of Tinkling Springs Presbyterian Church. JILLSON's Kentucky Land Grants.

Jefferson Co, KY Marriages From Feb. 16, 1784 to June 28, 1826, Vols. 1-2.

Virginia Military Warrants, by Willard R. JILLSON.

Early Kentucky Wills and Marriages, by Mrs. William Breckenridge ARDERY.

Family Bible records.http://cafamilies.org/finley/ancient-rts.html

http://cafamilies.org/finley/macbeth-rts.html#lorne

http://www.angelfire.com/biz/finleyfindings/

http://cafamilies.org/finley/clan_finley.html

http://irvinemclean.com/peerage/mar.htm

http://www.duffus.com/sundaynews9_2_00.htm

http://our-royal-titled-noble-and-commoner-ancestors.com/p234.htm

http://www.algerclan.org/getperson.php?personID=I117238&tree=alger

http://en.rodovid.org/wk/Person:142611

http://clanmaclochlainn.com/pedigree.htm

Celtic Scotland: a history of ancient Alban, Volume 3 By William Forbes Skene Pg. 477

http://www.magma.ca/mmackay/moray.html

http://forums.totalwar.org/vb/archive/

http://nobleworldchrono.9f.com/britishisles.htm

http://web.raex.com/obsidian/scot.html#Moray

MORE REFERENCES AND sources:

http://cafamilies.org/finley/ancient-rts.html

http://cafamilies.org/finley/macbeth-rts.html#lorne

http://www.angelfire.com/biz/finleyfindings/

http://cafamilies.org/finley/clan_finley.html

http://irvinemclean.com/peerage/mar.htm

http://en.rodovid.org/wk/Person:142611

http://clanmaclochlainn.com/pedigree.htm

Celtic Scotland: a history of ancient Alban, Volume 3 By William Forbes Skene Pg. 477